Folk Carving

with Shane Campbell

Text written with and photography
by Jeffrey B. Snyder

Schiffer Publishing Ltd
4880 Lower Valley Road, Atglen, PA 19310 USA

Dedication

In memory of my father and favorite southern folk artist, Jack Campbell. The spirit of his work lives on. I also wish to dedicate this book to my wife Nancy. Without her encouragement, patience, and understanding (not to mention painting skills), this book would have never happened, because I would be working at a *real* job instead of what I love.

Contents

Library of Congress Catalog Card Number: 97-80467

Book Design by Laurie A. Smucker

ISBN: 0-7643-0465-8
Printed in United States

Published by Schiffer Publishing Ltd.
4880 Lower Valley Road
Atglen, PA 19310
Phone: (610) 593-1777; Fax: (610) 593-2002
E-mail: schifferbk@aol.com
Please write for a free catalog.
This book may be purchased from the publisher.
Please include $3.95 for shipping.
Try your bookstore first.

We are interested in hearing from authors with book ideas on related subjects.

Introduction

As this is my first attempt at a carving book and I am basically self-taught (except for a few pointers from my father along the way), I wanted to keep it simple, while trying to add in a little fun. After all, folk art is supposed to be fun. The best folk art I have ever seen was not perfect, but naive and primative and made me smile. The designs in this book are simple, yet when completed have the qualities of the afore-mentioned, with the flavor of Early Americana -- things made by hand -- fun things made from the heart. So remember the only rule you have to follow is this: *there are no rules*. Relax and enjoy ...

If I may be of additional help or inspiration, please write to me at:

The Workshop
7000 S. Dent Road
Hixson, TN 37343

For replys, please include an SASE (self addressed, stamped envelope). Remember -- I am always at home, except when I'm not!

Materials Needed

One good carving knife,
a #2 flat gouge,
a #7 bent gouge,
a #8 fish tail gouge,
any V gouge,
a drill or drill press,
and a small hammer.

Finishes Needed

Black Primer in a spray can
DAP caulking compound
Latex paint
and Briwax

Carving An Angel Named Ruby

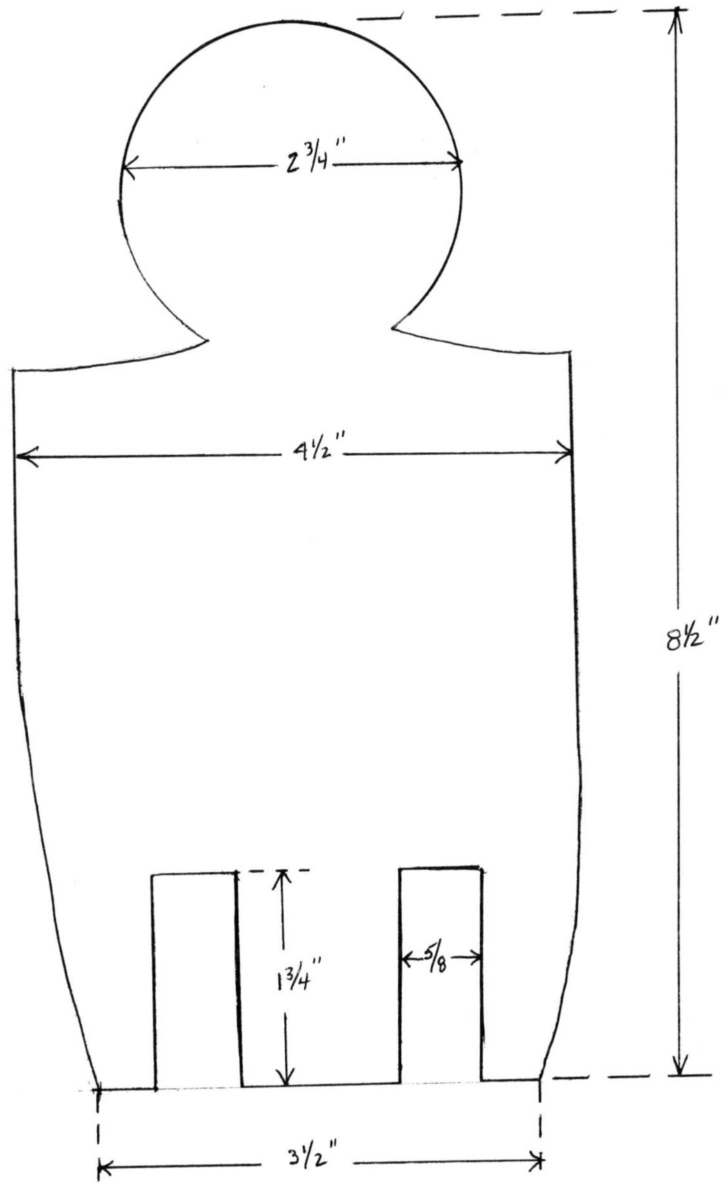

Pattern shown reduced to 65%.

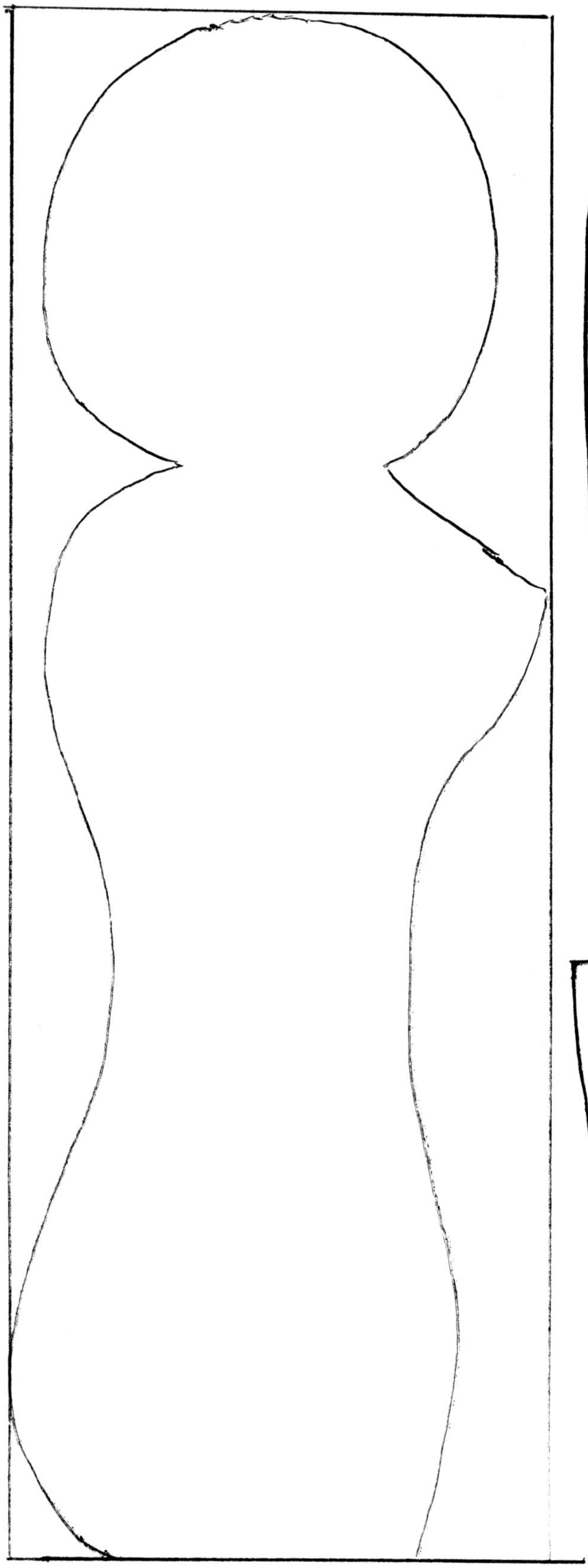

"Ruby" profile, 3" stock Actual size.

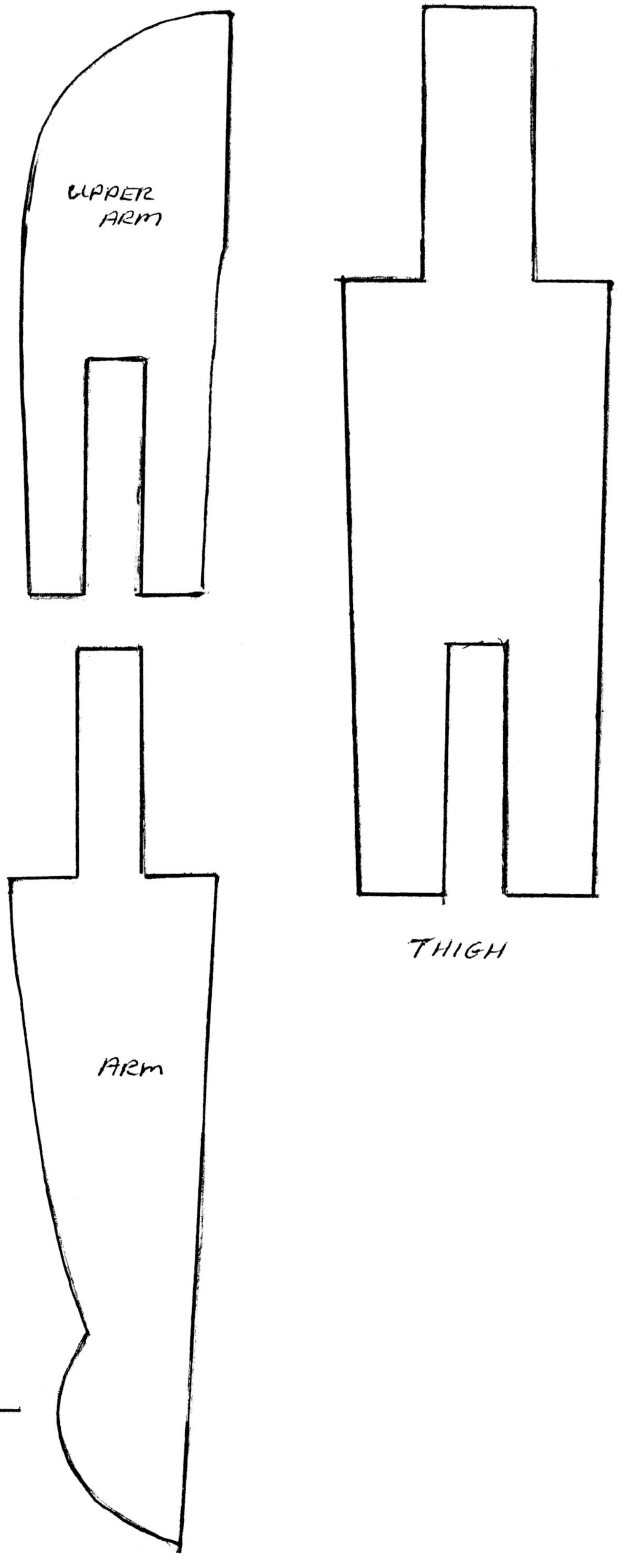

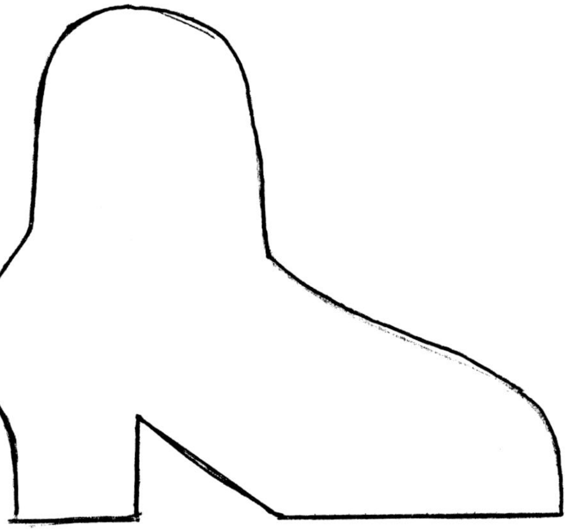

LOWER LEG

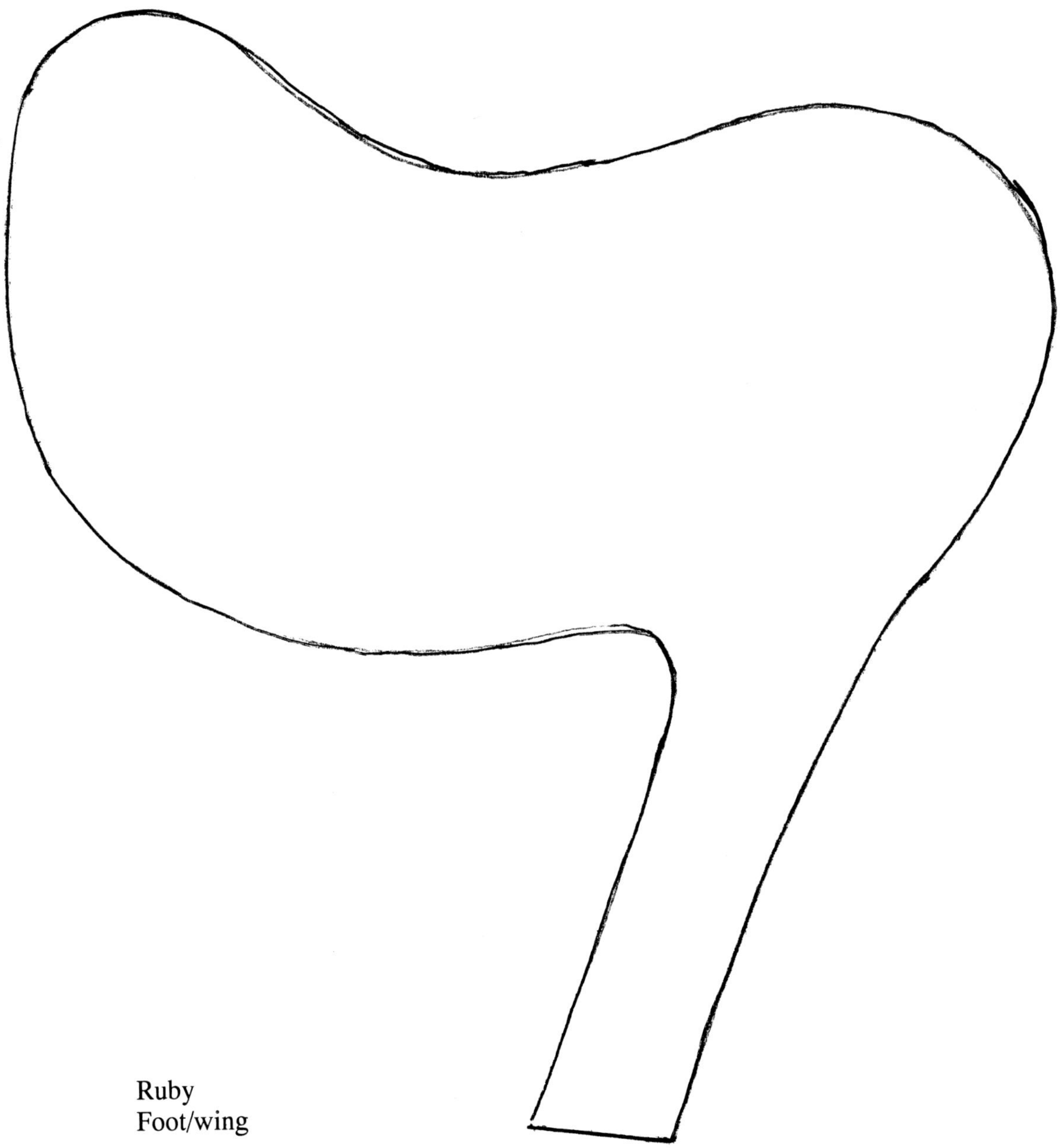

Ruby
Foot/wing

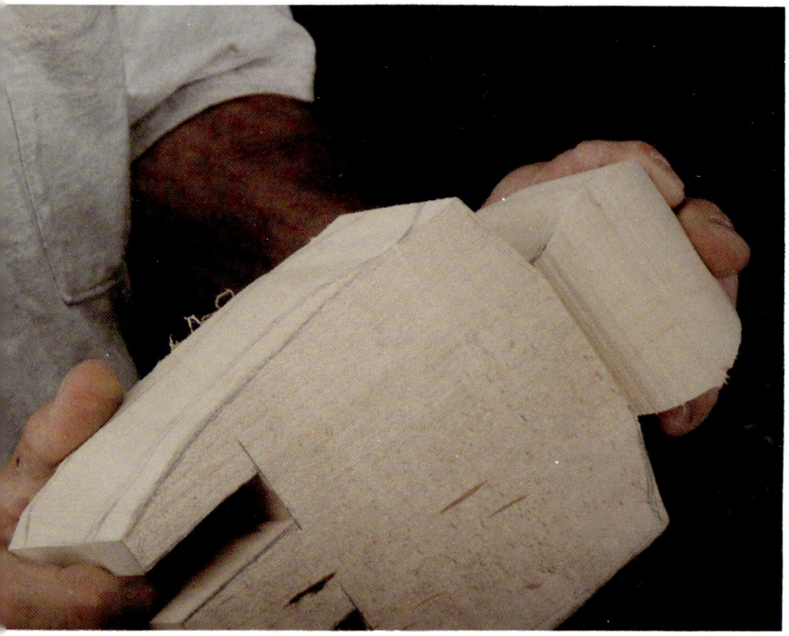

Trace the profile onto the side of the body block. It is important to note that while cutting the profile, the bandsaw blade must be perpendicular to the breasts. If not, one will be larger than the other. Everywhere else, there is plenty of extra wood to allow for a margin of error. Before I begin cutting, I kiss the blade to the wood where I wish to cut to make sure that the kerf (the mark left by the blade) is perpendicular to the breast line. This mark will ensure that your work is square. The reason for this check is that you have already begun to roughly shape the block and it is no longer square. It is advisable not to drink moonshine during this process.

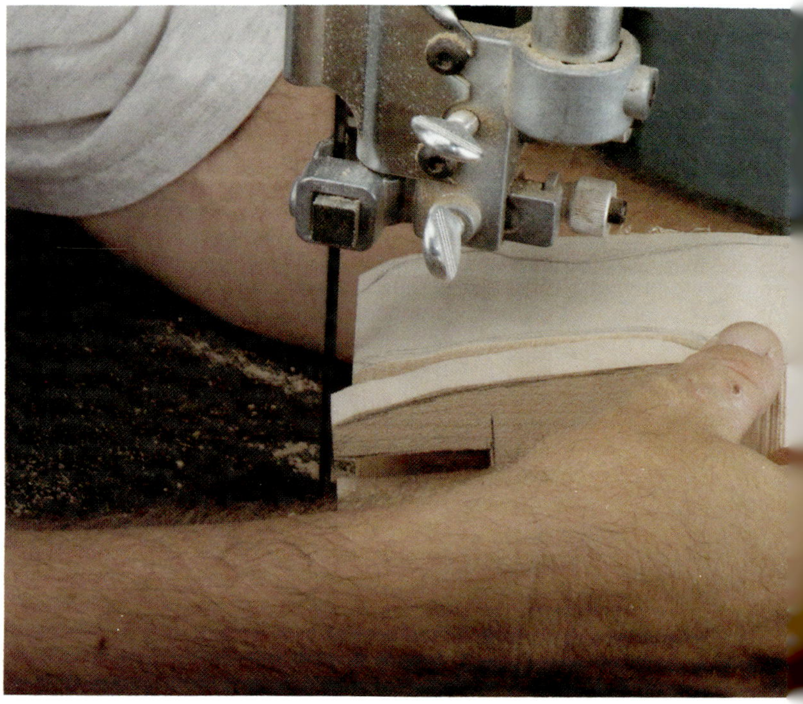

Cutting the profile.

After the initial profile cuts were made on the bandsaw, I noticed that this angel's body was a little wide. If this happens, use the bandsaw to narrow her down a bit.

Cutting down the profile.

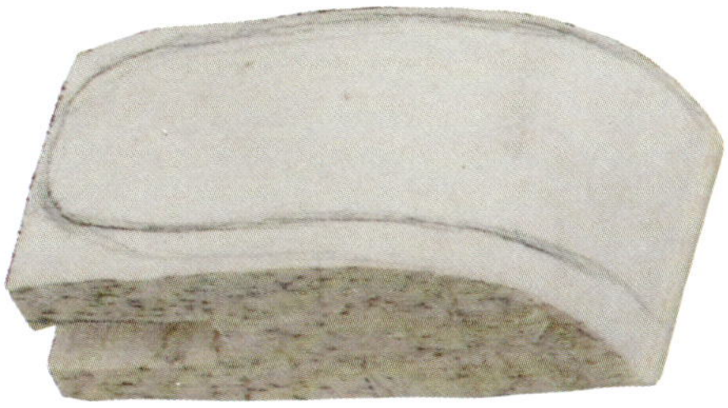

Cut out the remaining pieces for the arms, legs, and feet. They are half way done as shown here. Follow the pattern lines and finish them. These pieces include the upper arm ...

the lower arm ...

the thigh ...

the lower leg ...

and the foot.

At this point it is a good idea to trim down the fitted parts. The wood is less thick here and a more accurate cut can now be obtained.

As you cut, make sure your tenons are long enough for the limb to bend naturally. This leg tenon is long enough for the leg to bend at the knee far enough to ensure a natural seated position.

Checking the fit of the arm joint. The lower arm tenon fits into the cut in the upper arm well.

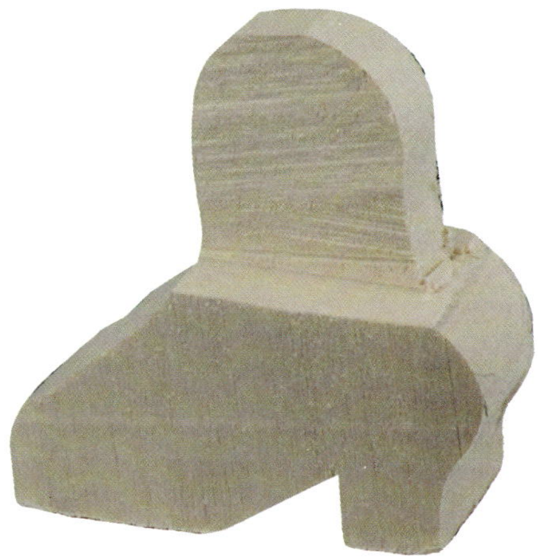

The shoe is now roughed out.

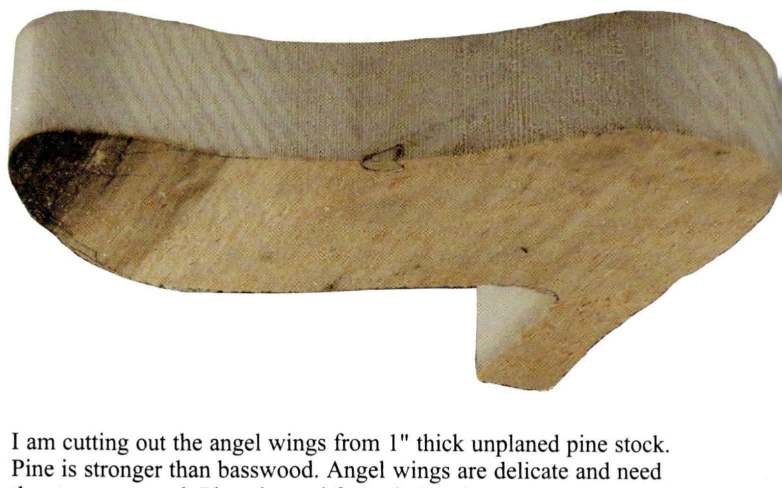

I am cutting out the angel wings from 1" thick unplaned pine stock. Pine is stronger than basswood. Angel wings are delicate and need the stronger wood. Planed wood from the lumber yard would only be 3/4" thick and always costs more. So I use the rough, unplaned stock. Once the basic angel wing outline is cut on the bandsaw, draw a center line and cut the wing in half to create two wings.

The centerline is in place.

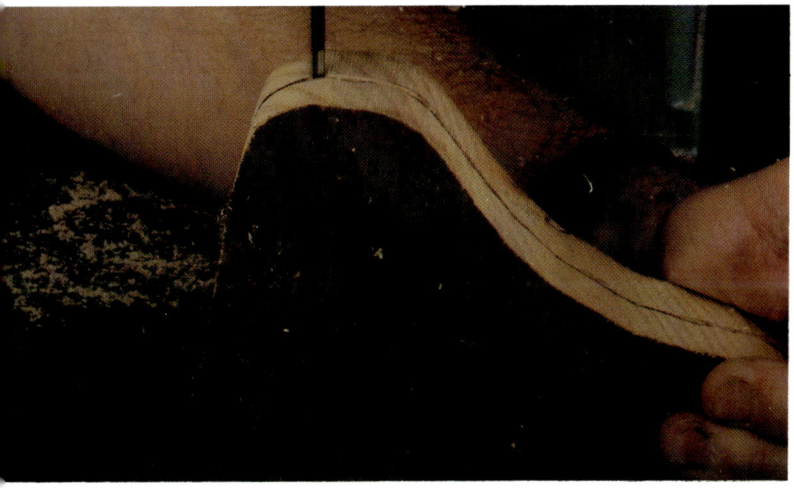

Cutting the wings in half.

The wings have been cut.

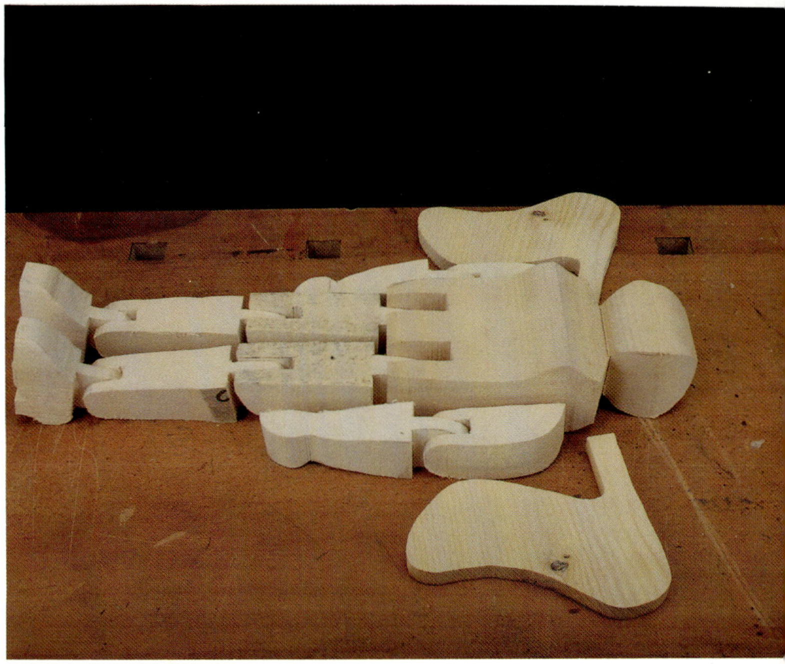

All of the roughed out parts for Ruby are here, ready for carving.

To begin carving, start rounding the head.

Continue rounding the head. Looking down on the work from the top of the head will help you determine if you are keeping the head in proportion all the way around.

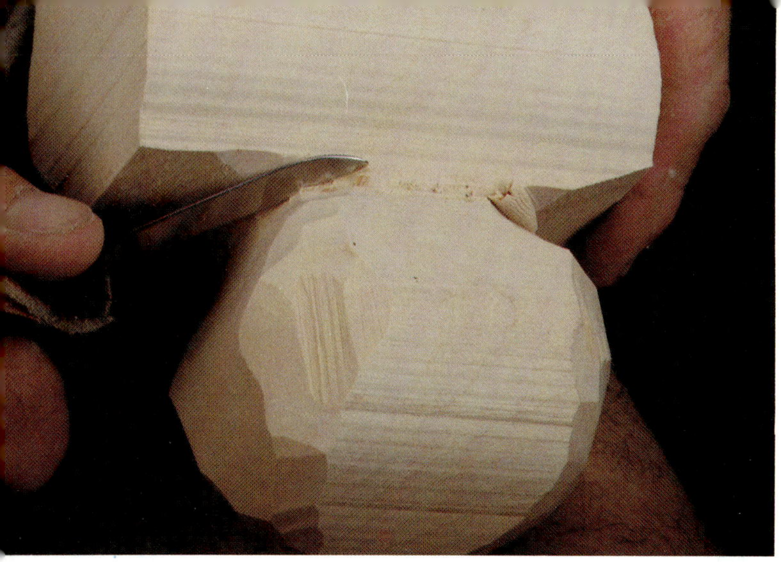

Make a V cut at the base of the head to define the neck.

Continuing to round the head. It is better to leave extra wood in place when cutting the blank and to take off the excess with a knife than to take off too much too soon and have to start over.

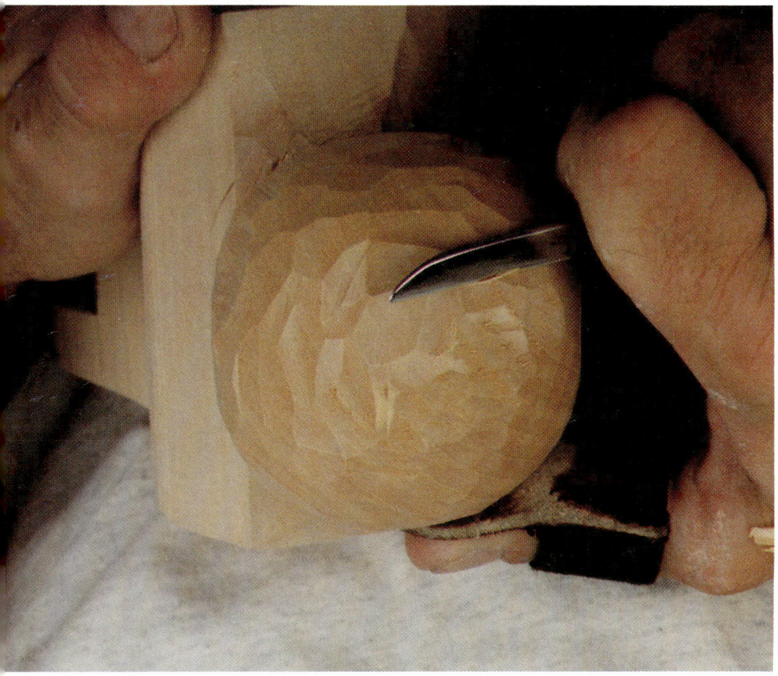

The head is taking shape.

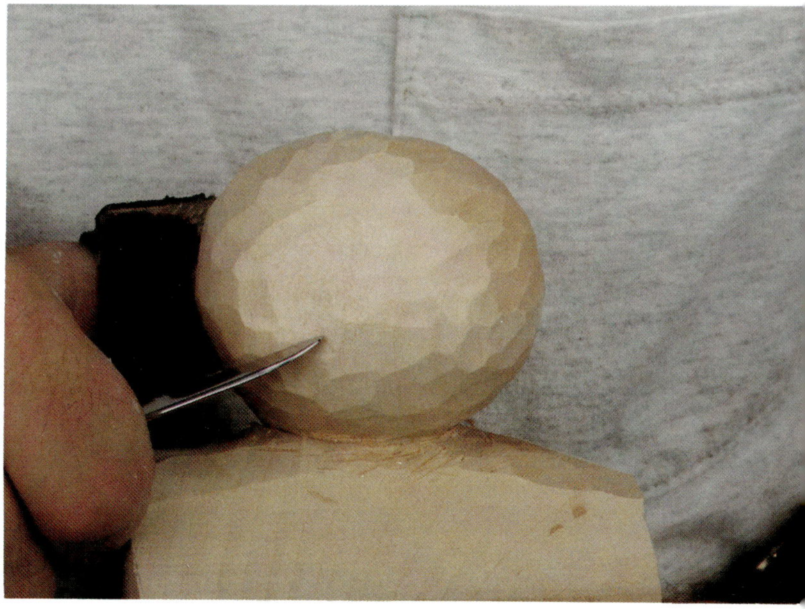

The head is now rounded. Get the head rounded until it looks good to you. Don't try for a perfect circle because the human head isn't completely round. Also, make sure that all of the saw marks have been removed in the rounding process.

The head was off center a bit from the beginning. We were able to compensate for that by carving the neck closer to center even though the head is off a bit. Now it appears correct. Being a little off in folk carving is not usually a problem.

Begin rounding down the sharp edges on the body. Make the shoulders rounded on the back and round in the breasts a bit.

Using the bench knife, make a stop cut down the line we drew in for the cleavage.

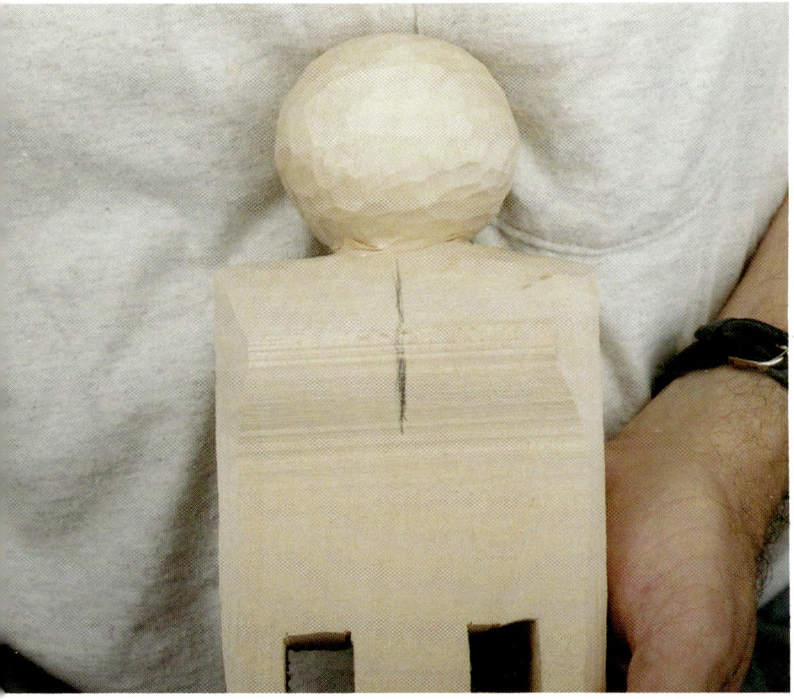

This is as much rounding in as the breasts need until you move in to work on the cleavage.

Make a V shaped cut into the stop cut line.

Rounding the shoulders in back.

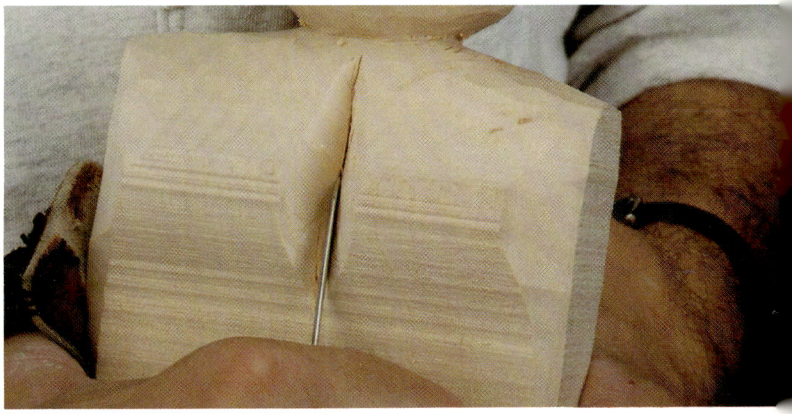

Repeat along the line of the other breast.

Do some initial rounding of the edges of the breasts with the bench knife. A chisel will finish the job later.

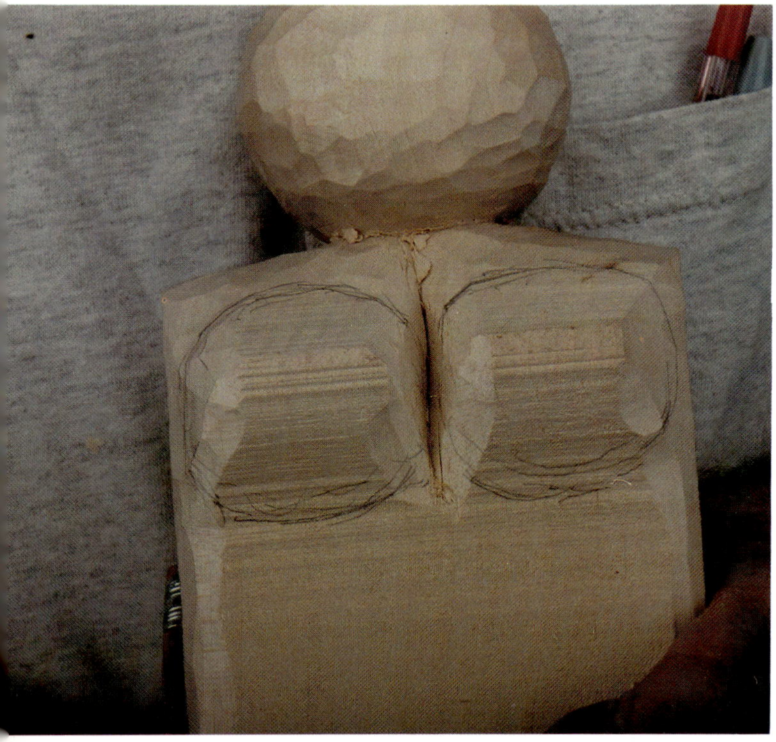

Once you have generally rounded off the breasts, draw circles around them as guides to follow with your chisel.

This is as much rounding as you need to do with the bench knife (both in front and behind). We will round further with a flat gouge. Remember, you are making folk art here. The work is supposed to be fun and relaxing. Perfection is not something to aim for. Small mistakes add character and are perfectly acceptable. If it seems tedious, you are trying too hard!

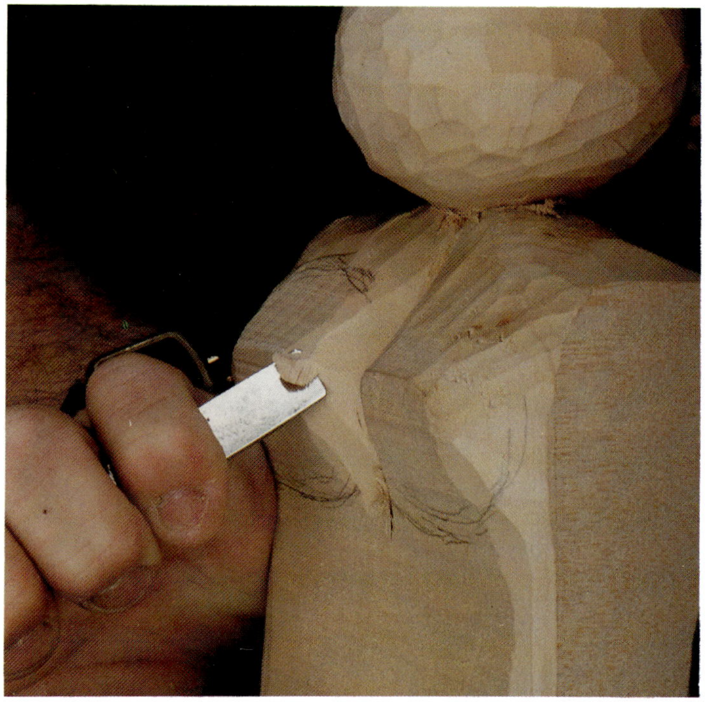

Round out the breast with the gouge. Mainly we're working on the four corners, rounding them down and out toward our circular guide lines. A straight gouge works fine for the tops of the breasts.

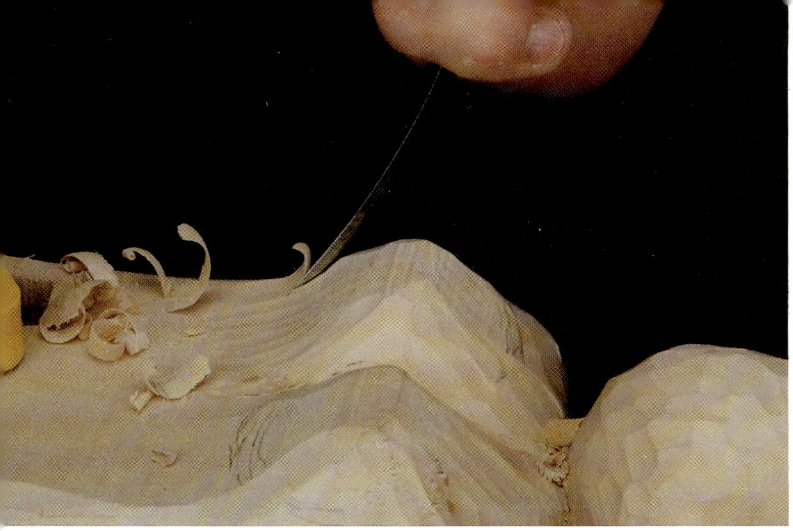

Use a bent gouge to round off the bottoms of the breasts. This provides a nice sweeping curve into the body and does not split the wood as a straight gouge would in this area.

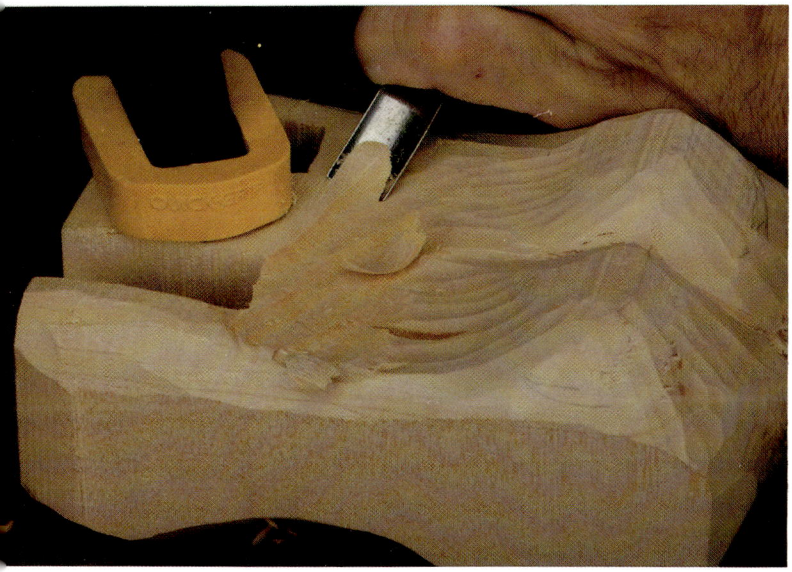

In the lower torso, cut across the grain to limit the amount of wood removed. It is important to remove the saw marks at this stage and not to remove large amounts of wood. If you go with the grain here you will split the wood and take out a big chunk.

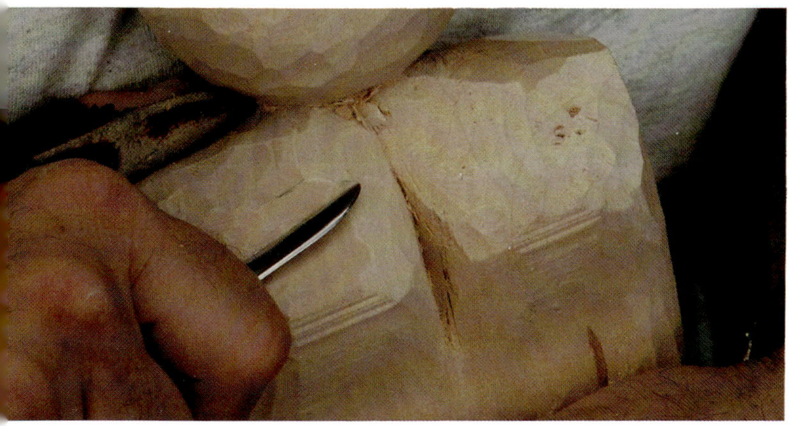

Further round the breasts with your bench knife, removing sharp edges and saw marks.

Take out a valley in between the shoulder blades on the back. Any time you use the gouge, it is important to keep your hand cupped over the gouge and your palm on either the work bench or the piece itself. This will give you more control with the gouge and will keep from slipping and gouging the back of the head when you put on too much pressure. This is a good practice any time you are using a gouge.

The valley between the shoulder blades is now in place. It is carved in deep enough when it is level with the back of the neck.

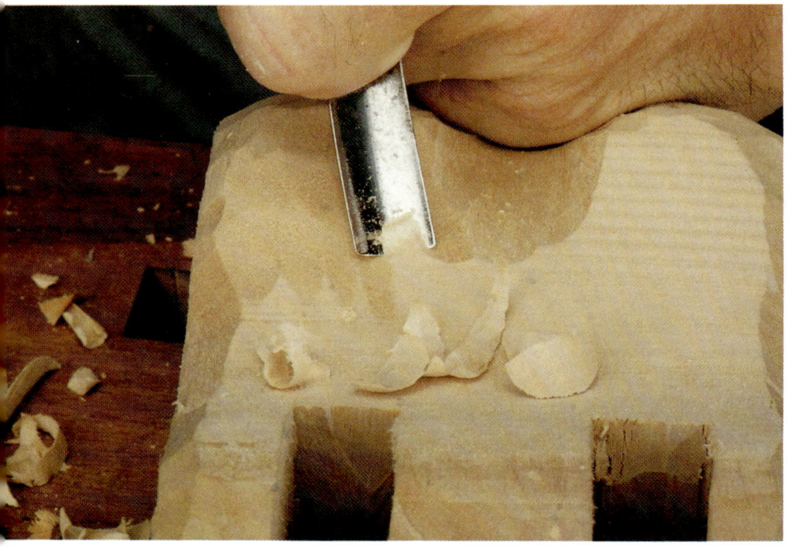

Rounding off the back, getting rid of the saw marks, rounding out the edges of the valley between the shoulder blades, and generally removing the least wood possible.

The upper back is rounded. Now change directions and round across the lower back.

Cut across the grain in the small of the back. If you don't, you will split the wood at the base of the spine.

Now the figure is generally rounded. It is time for some detail work. The breasts are still pretty square. It is time to refine them. Continue to cut deep into the cleavage to retain this strong line as you round.

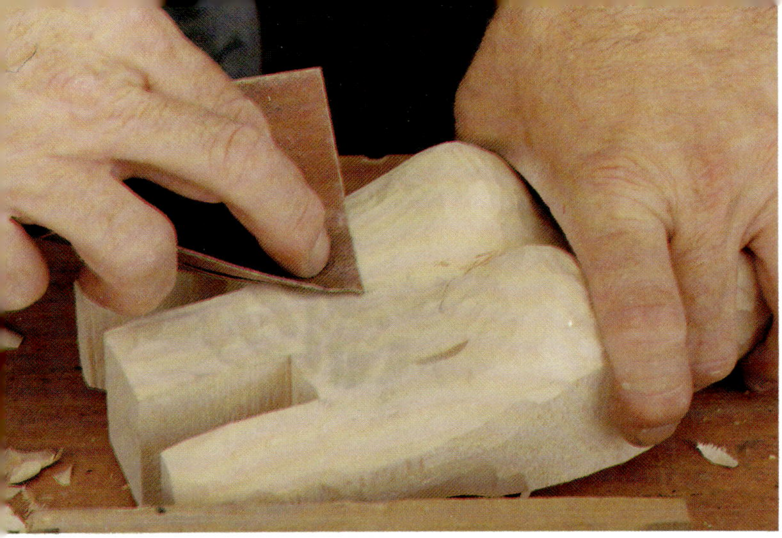

The body is rounded down. I prefer to sand as little as possible. However, I need to sand in the areas of the cross grain cuts to remove the rough edges.

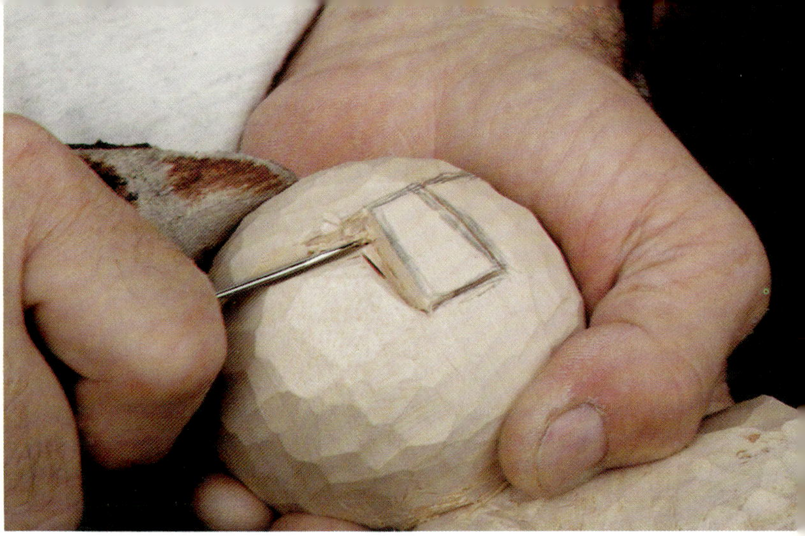

Angle cuts into the incised lines to begin to remove wood from around the nose and eyes.

I have drawn in the outline of the brow line and the nose. These are the highest points on the face and will act as my guides.

Angled cuts have been made back into the incised cuts around the eyebrows and nose.

Incise straight in along these lines with the bench knife.

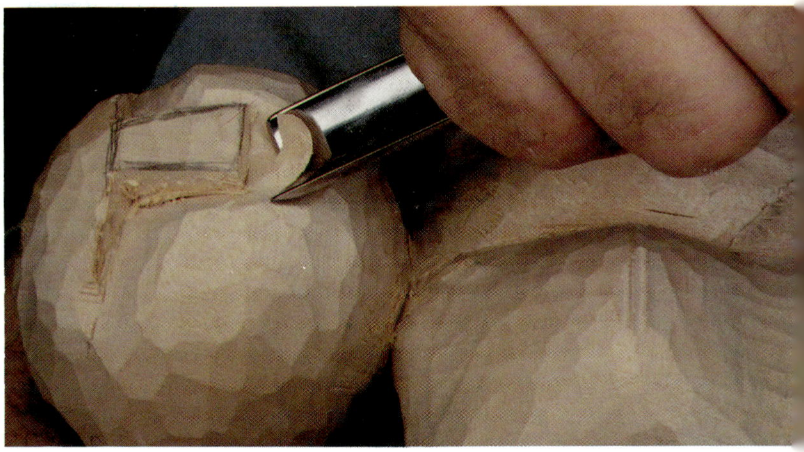

Make two or three swipes with a fishtail gouge up into the bottom of the nose to further expose this area and to flatten out the mouth. The fishtail gouge will also keep the cheeks high and rounded, adding character.

Like so.

Scallop out below the cheeks with the bench knife, down to the level of the mouth.

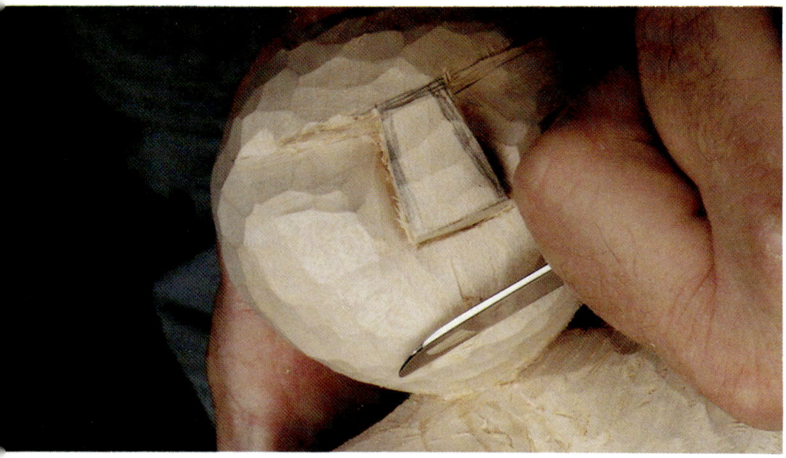

Work to remove some of the sharp lines of the chin with the bench knife.

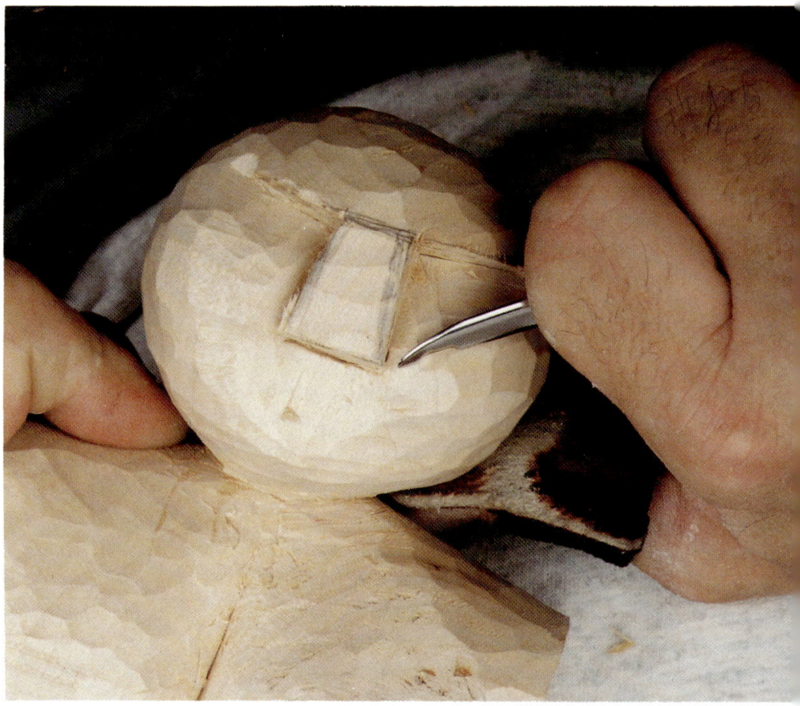

Round out the cheeks, taking all the sharp edges off. However, leaving the carving marks is fine. This gives the piece a desirable primitive look.

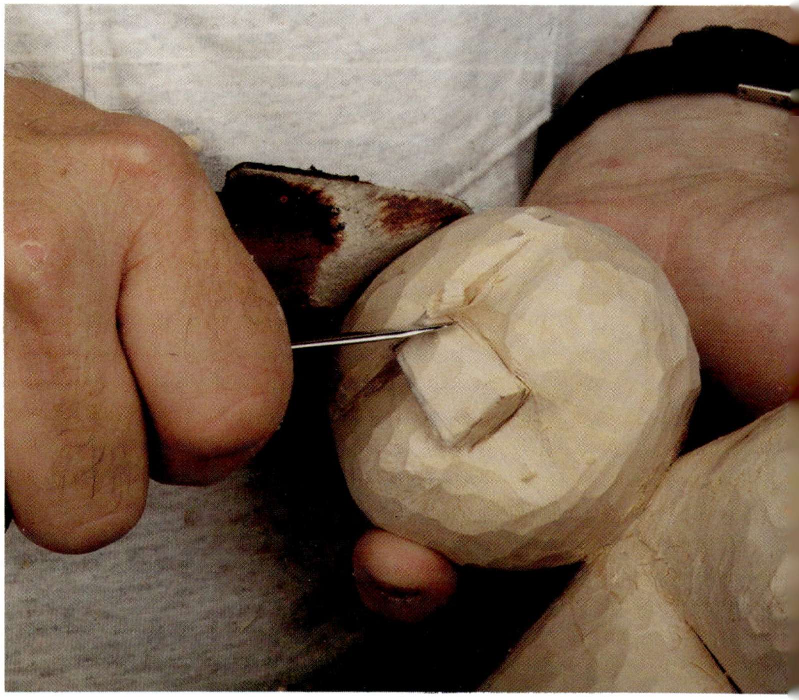

Round the edges of the nose and the eyebrows.

The face is rounded now. Clean up around the nose and mouth area prior to carving in the mouth itself.

Draw in the mouth. It should have a smile because folk art is fun!

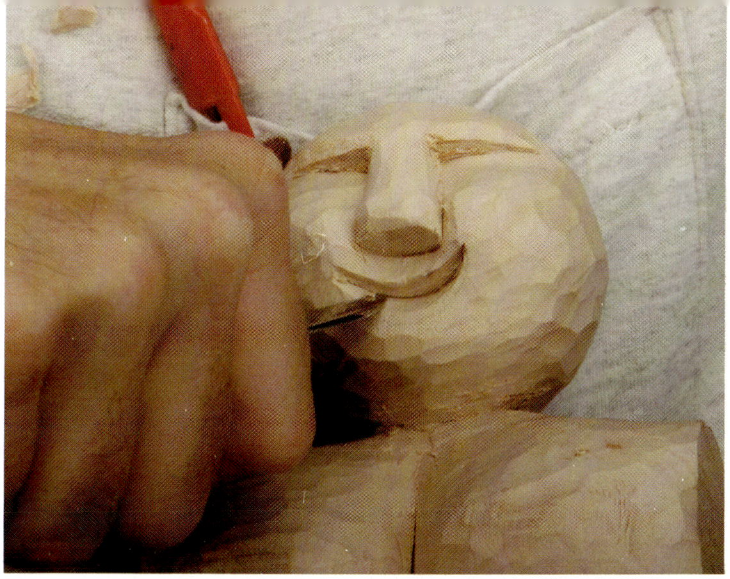

Use the bench knife to make a simple V cut to define the mouth. That is all there is to it.

Incise lines for the nostrils (place these lines at about the point your finger would stop if you put it up your nose) and narrow down the nose a bit with the bench knife.

Narrowing the nose a bit down to the incised line of the nostril. Now the nostrils are raised up above the rest of the nose.

The completed face. Eyes and other details will be painted on later.

Draw in the neck line. I prefer a squared line along the back, but it can be rounded if you wish.

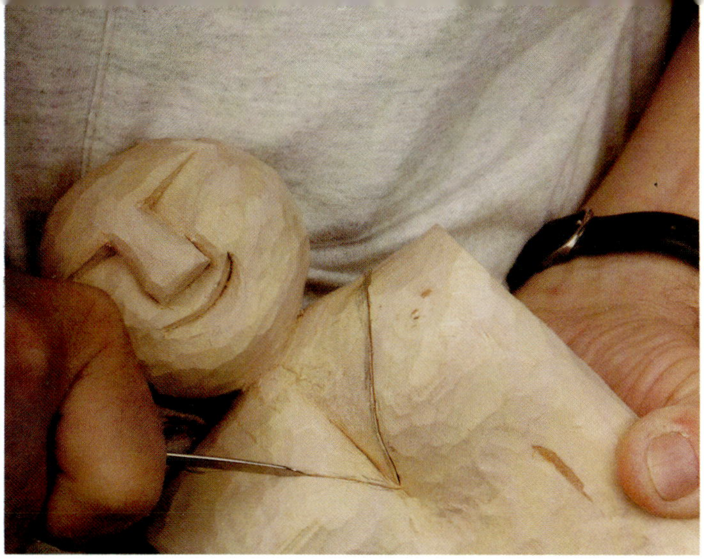

Cut straight in over the neck line.

Go back and angle in slightly up to the incised line to create a little depth for the neck and chest. This will leave the dress higher than the neck and create proper perspective.

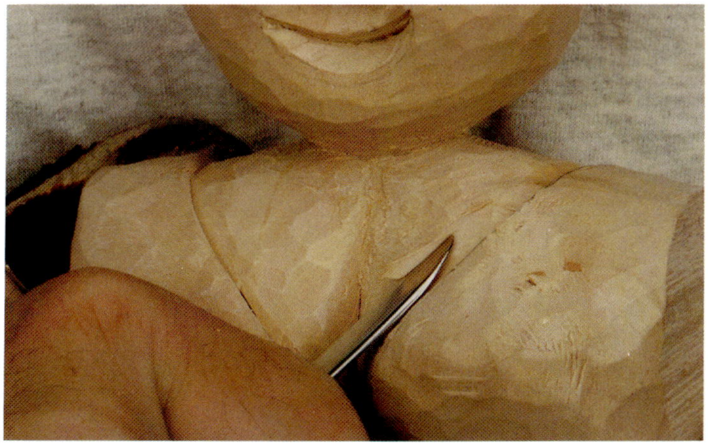

Round down the exposed neck and shoulders above the neck line with the bench knife. If you find there are areas you have trouble reaching with the knife, switch to a gouge.

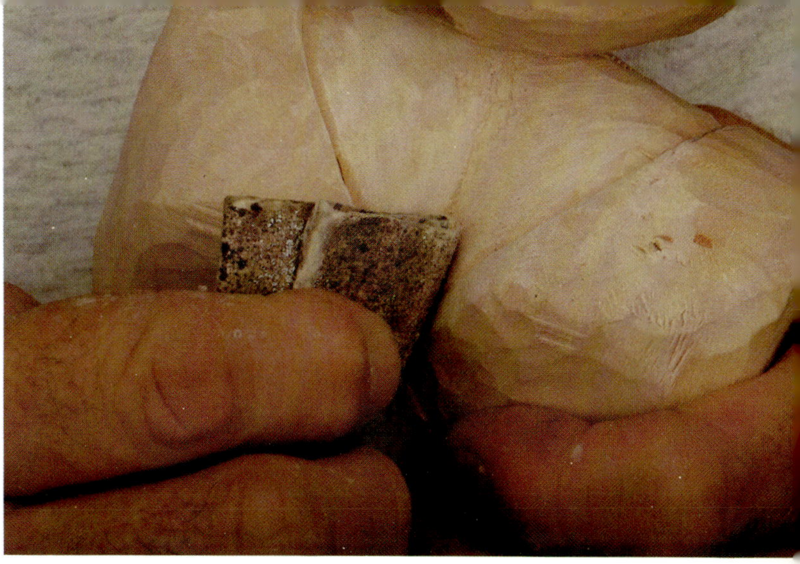

Use a little 100 grit sandpaper to remove rough areas and round the neck and cleavage.

Use a small V gouge to add some vertical lines to the dress, providing folds and character.

At the base of the back, you will have to reverse course and cut from the bottom up with the gouge. If you use just the right pressure, the same pressure as in the initial downward cut from above, the two will meet and appear to be a single, seamless line. This is the look you are shooting for.

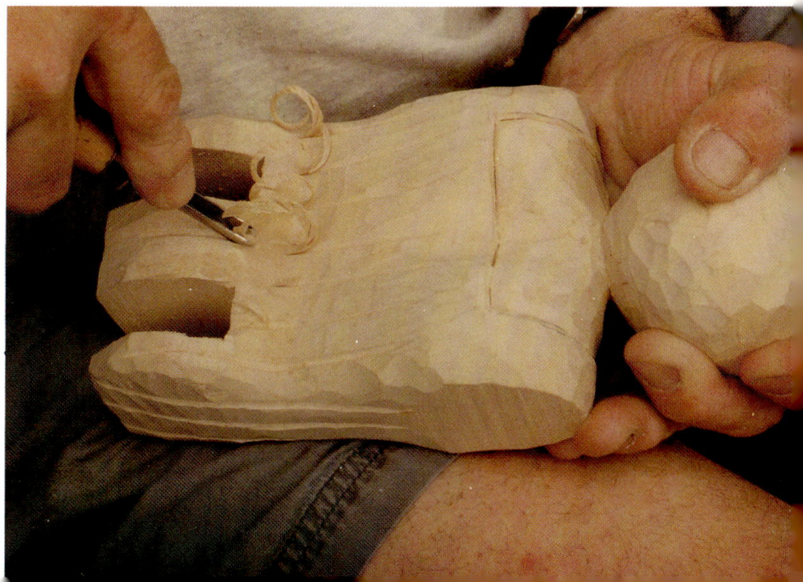

The lines are carved in for the dress. It is time to move on to the arms, legs, and wings.

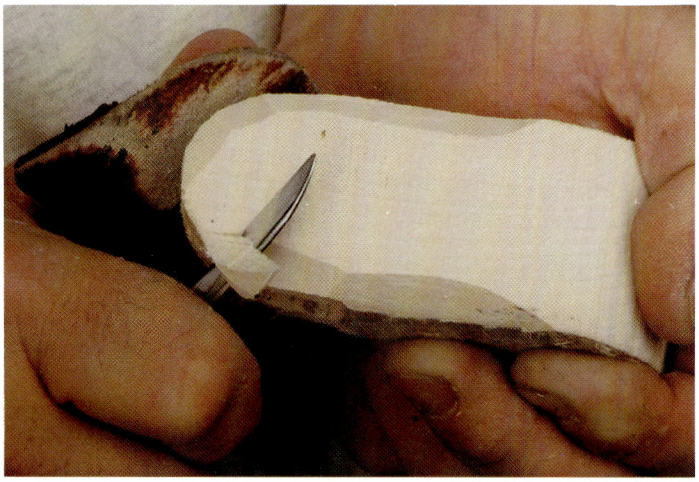

Begin rounding the inside and outside of the upper arm.

Round off the inside of the arm with the exception of the part that attaches to the side of the figure.

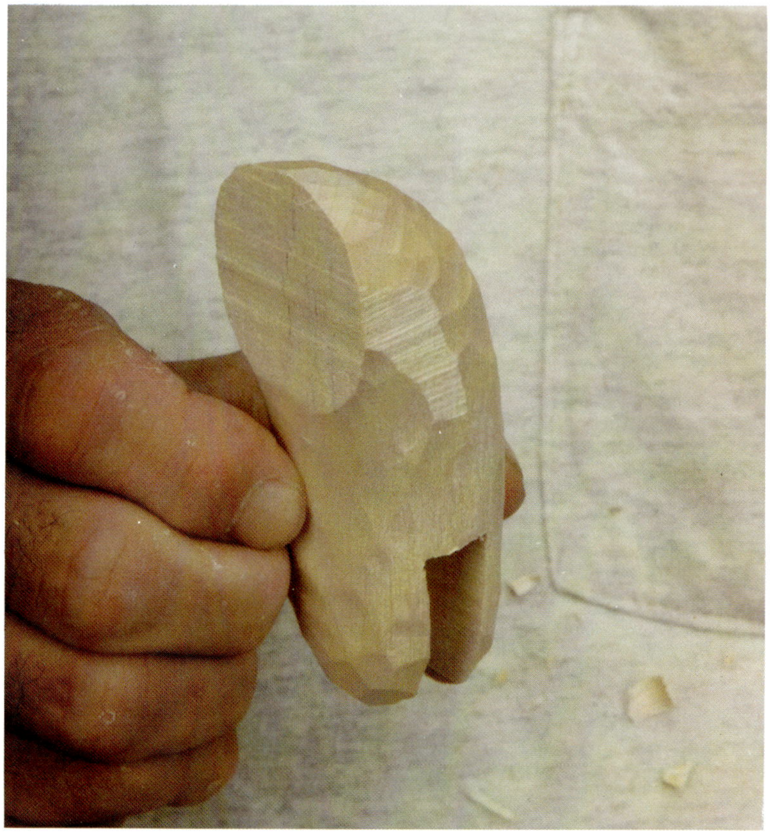

The upper arm is rounded.

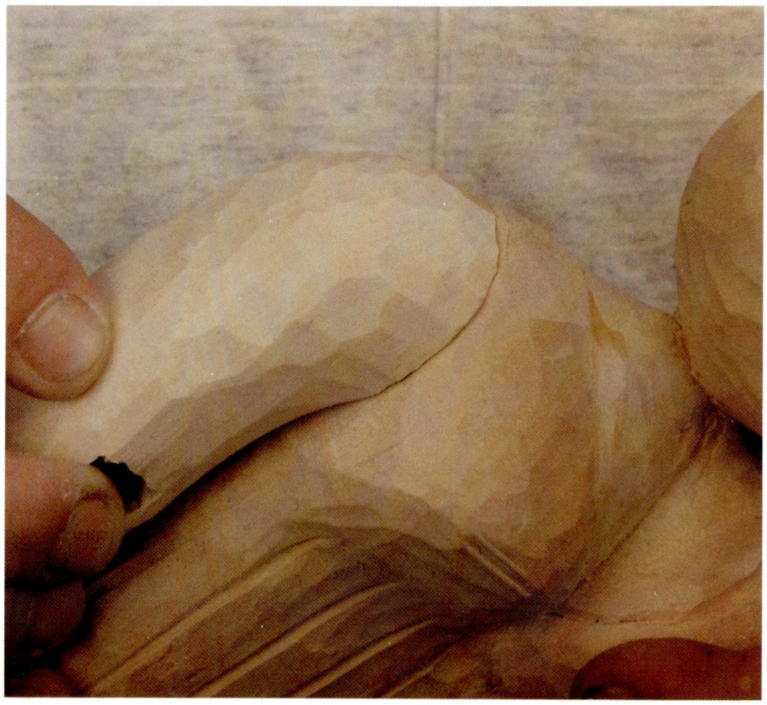

Checking the fit of the upper arm and the body.

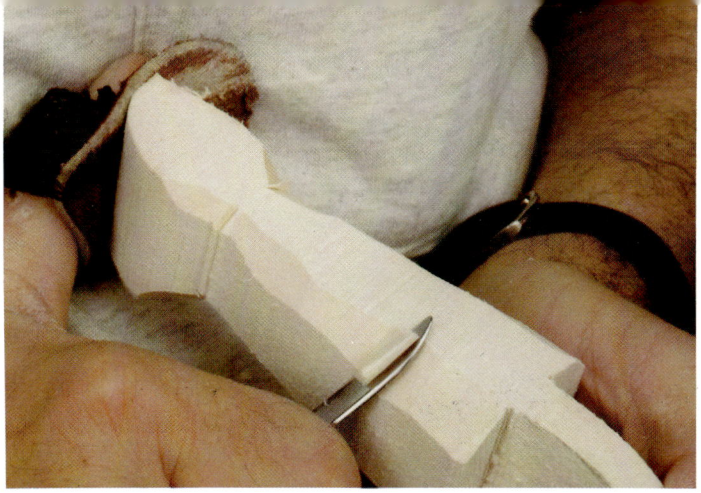

Rounding down the lower arm. Remember to make the upper part of the forearm the same thickness as the lower part of the upper arm.

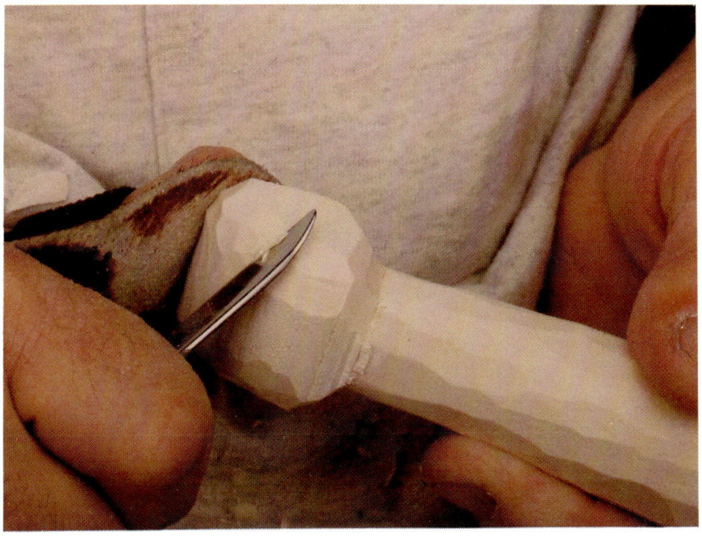

Gradually round down the hand.

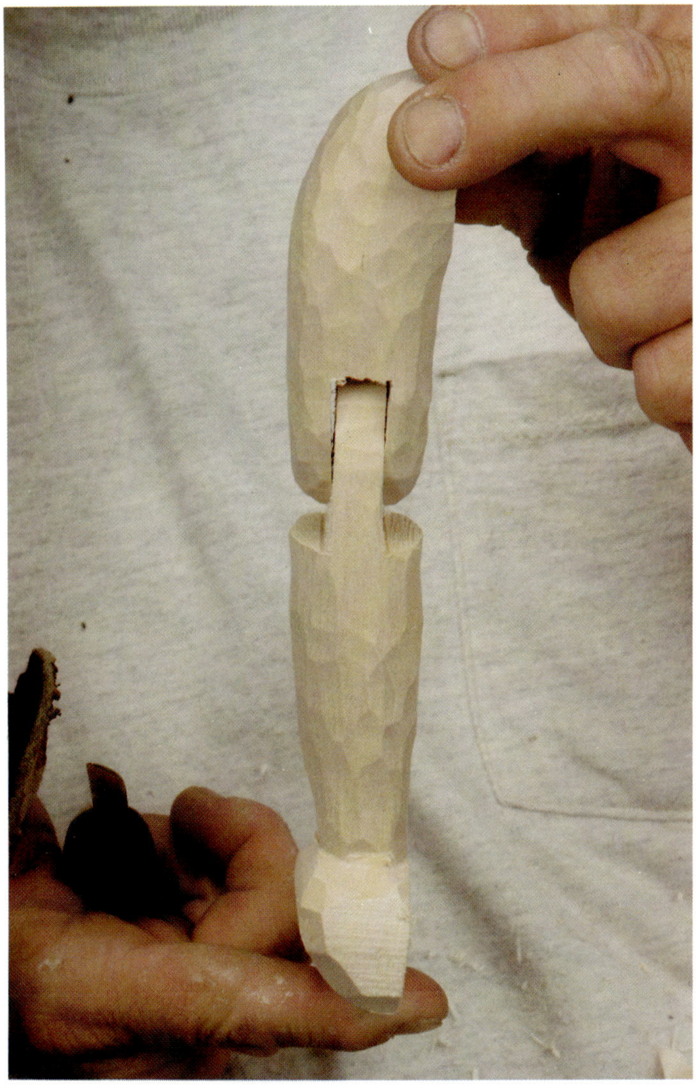

The upper part of the forearm is equal to the lower part of the upper arm in the side view. You want to make sure that the upper part of the lower arm is not wider than the upper arm. Both the upper and lower arm are now rounded. I wait until both arms are carved before I attempt to carve the hands. This way I can more easily size the hands, making sure one is not larger than the other.

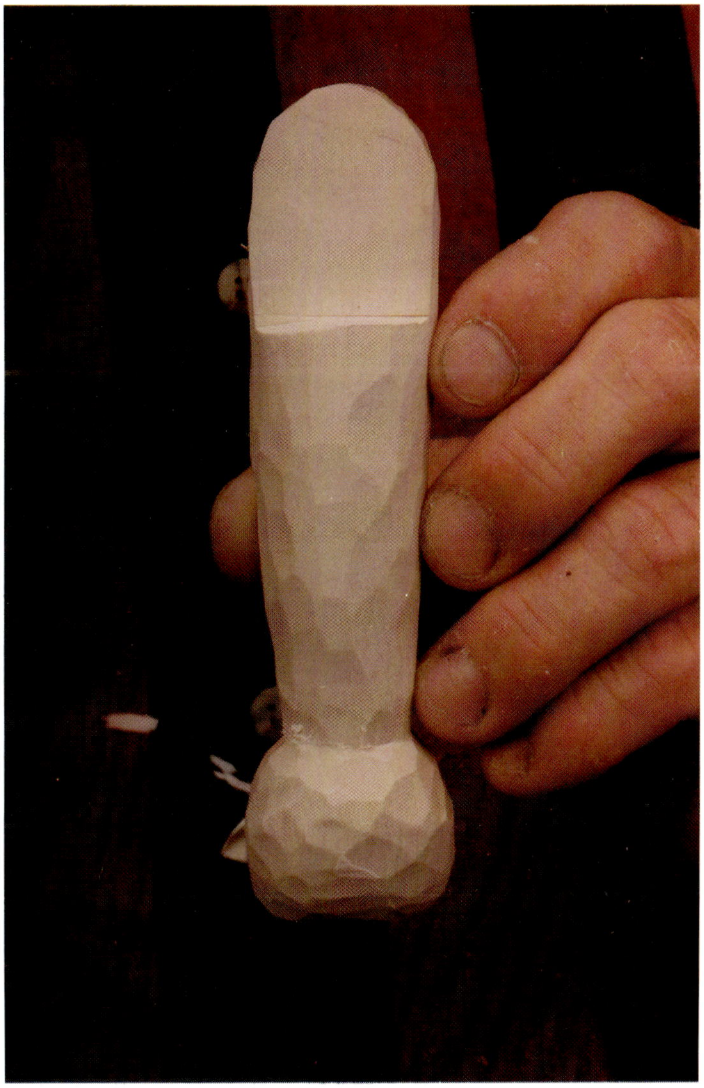

The hand and arm are now rounded. Make sure to round the other hand and arm before attempting to carve the fingers. It is worth repeating that this is an easy way to make sure both hands come out nearly the same size.

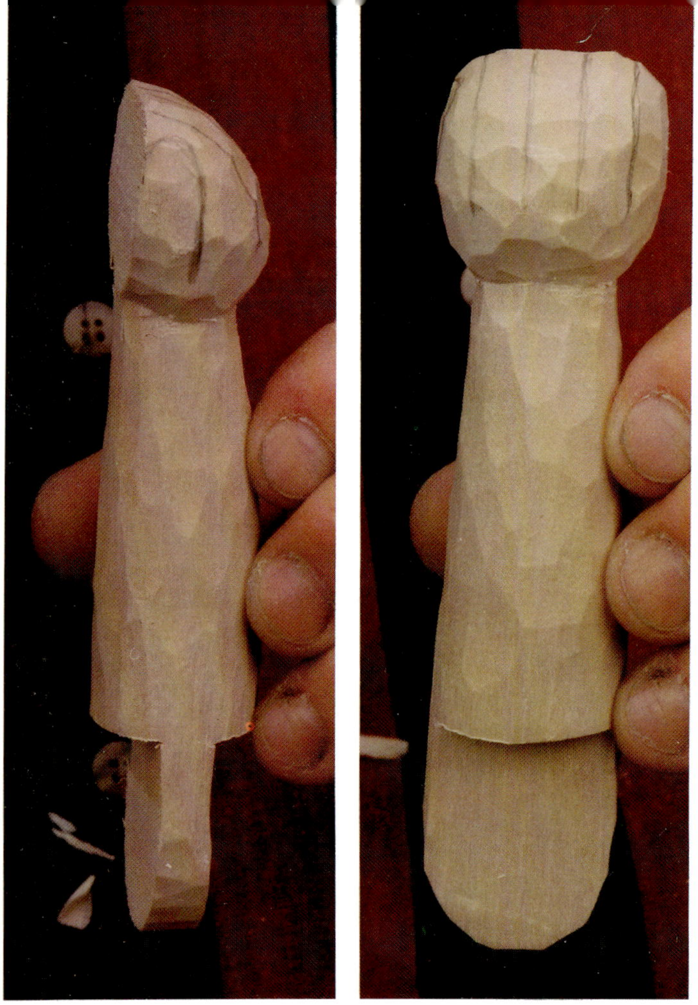

Mark fingers and the thumbs on both hands. Make sure to get the thumbs on the proper sides of the hands.

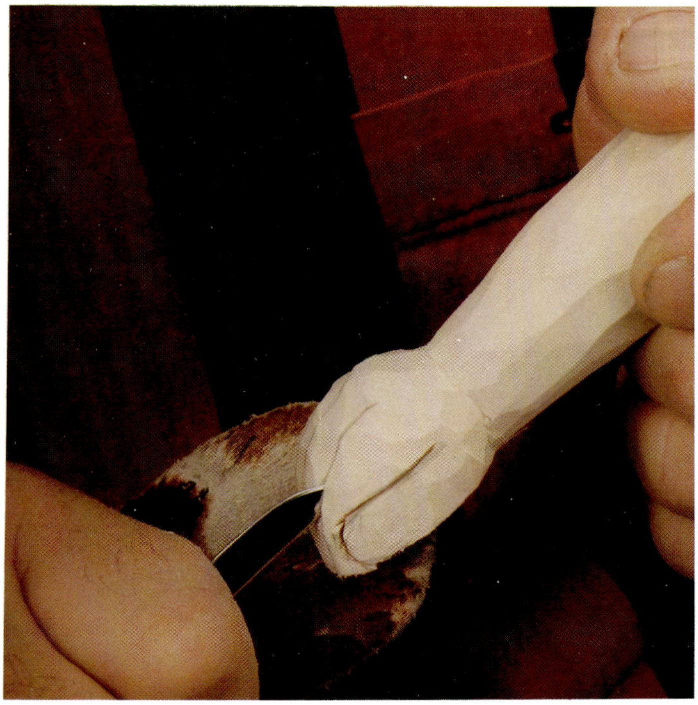

Using the bench knife, cut straight in to incise the lines of the fingers. With all the fingers except the forefingers, small V's will be removed from along the incised lines to separate the fingers.

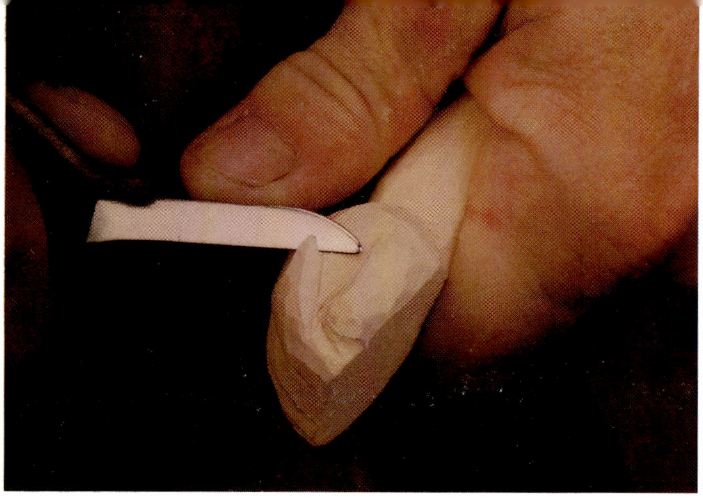

However, the area betweem the forefinger has the thumb needs to be reduced, raising the thumb and creating the gap in the closed hand, suggesting the curl of the fingers and the palm within.

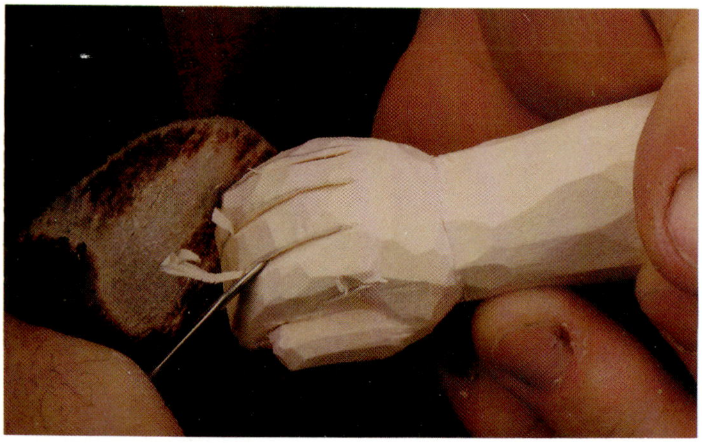

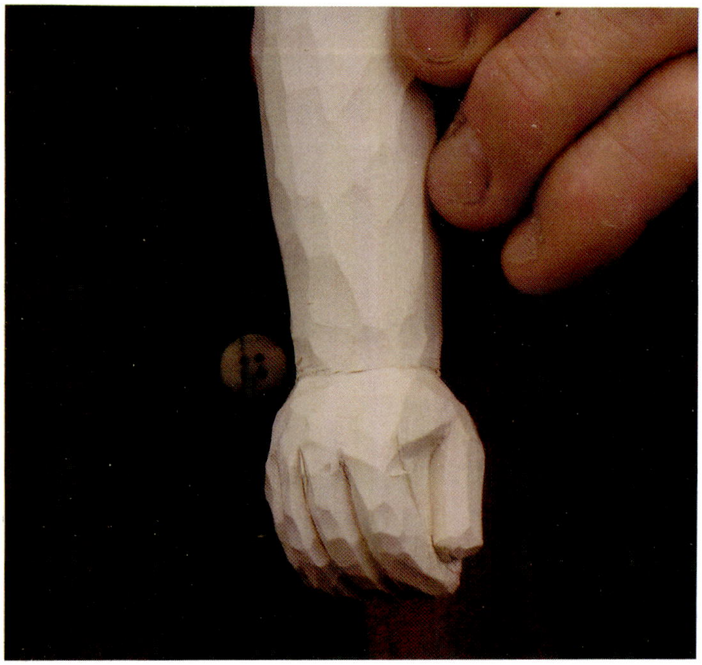

The small angled V cuts along both sides of the incised lines of the fingers look like this.

Make small V notches at the tips of the fingers. Cut from the underside of the hand. This will give the fingers a little extra definition.

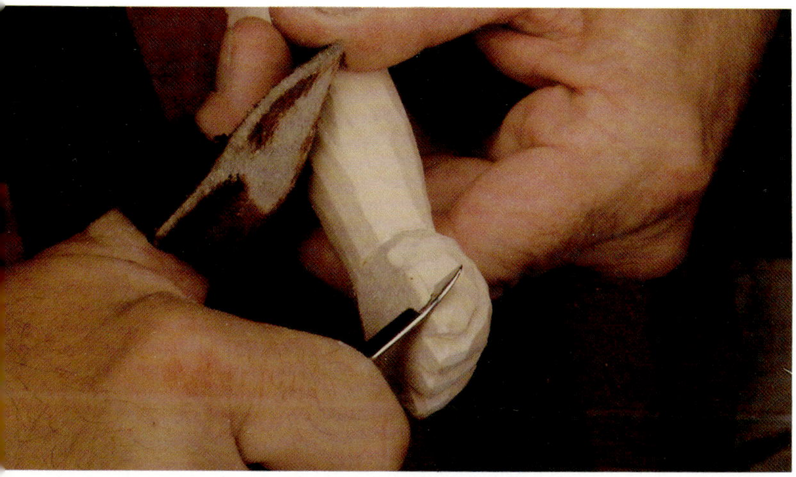

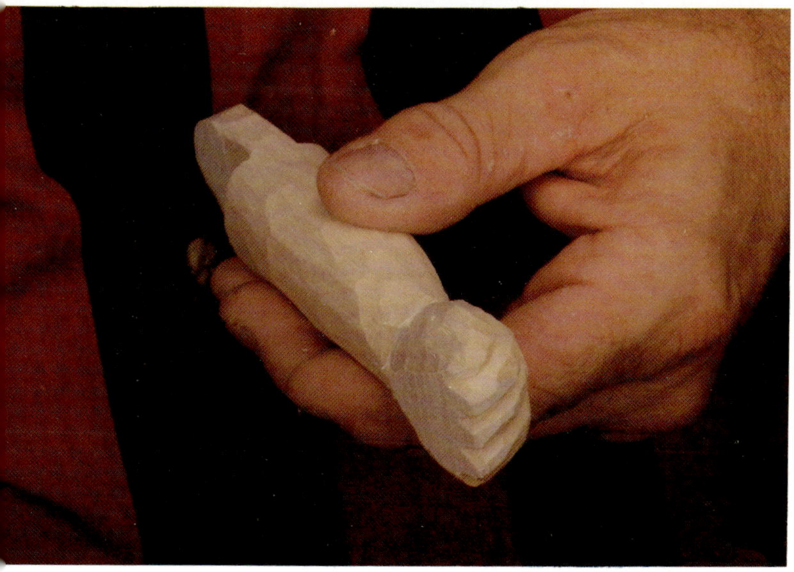

Remove some wood along the side and underneath of the little finger to further define it and add a little shape to the palm. The bench knife works well for this.

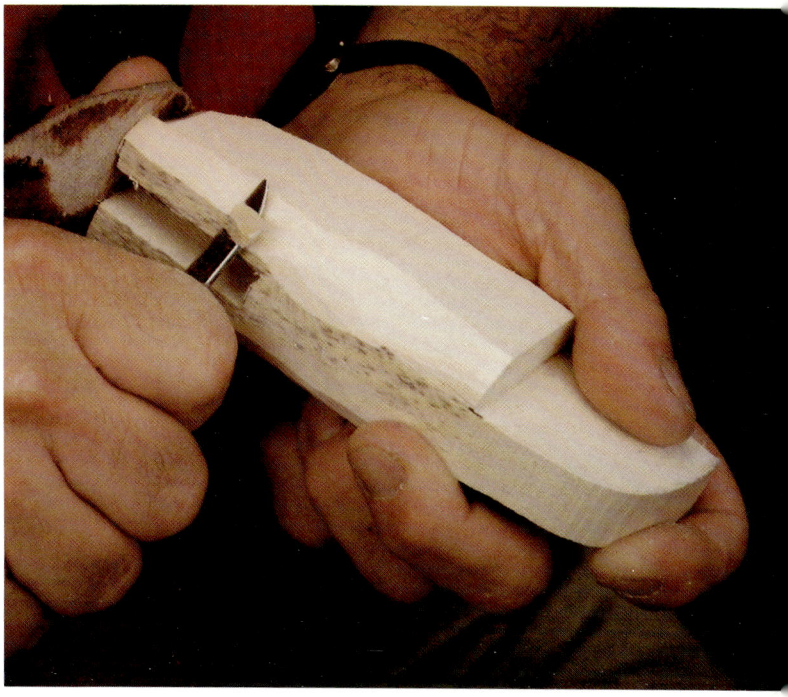

Begin rounding the thighs and lower legs now. Round the thighs together to make sure they are proportionally the same. We will repeat these steps with the lower legs as well.

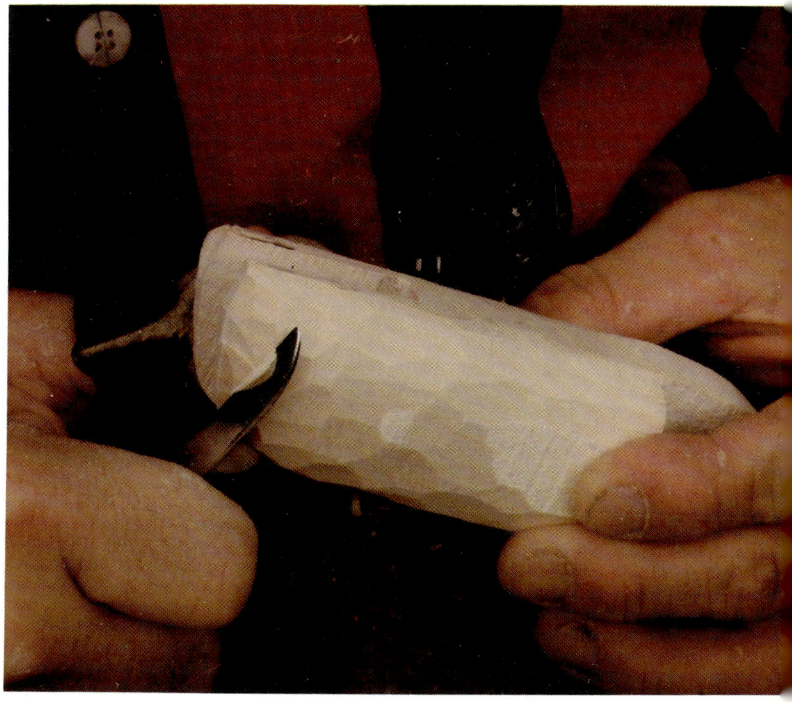

Taper down the ends at the joints to reduce the feeling of thickness and heaviness of the leg.

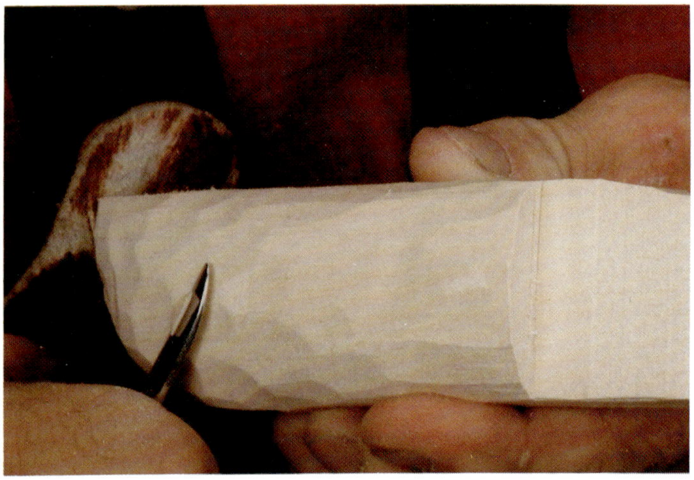

Don't bother to carve the insides of the joints as these will be hidden.

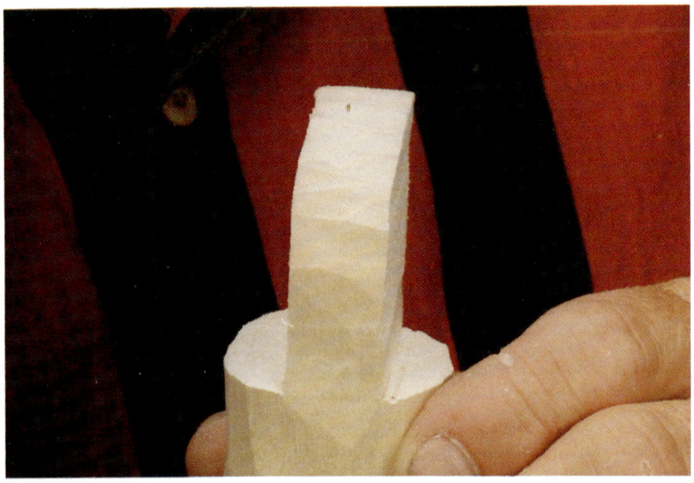

The rounded thigh.

Once the lower leg is rounded, check the joint with the upper leg. Make sure that the upper part of the lower leg is the same thickness as the lower part of the upper leg above the joint.

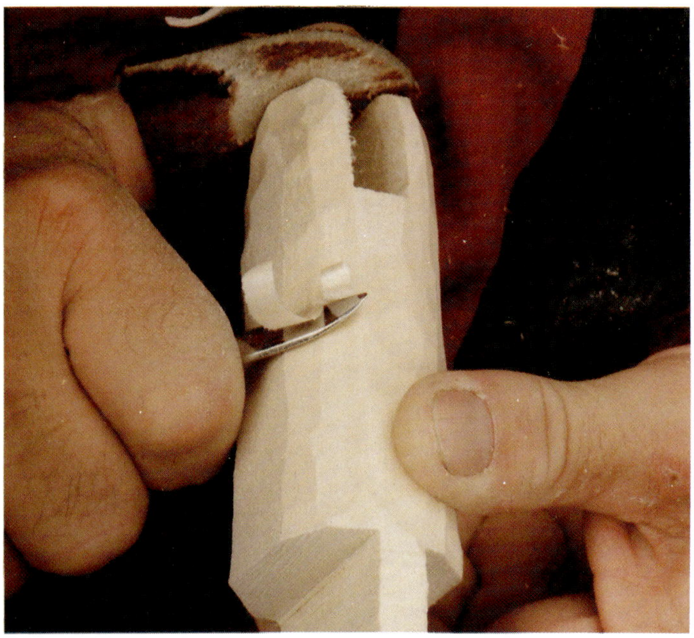

Rounding the lower leg.

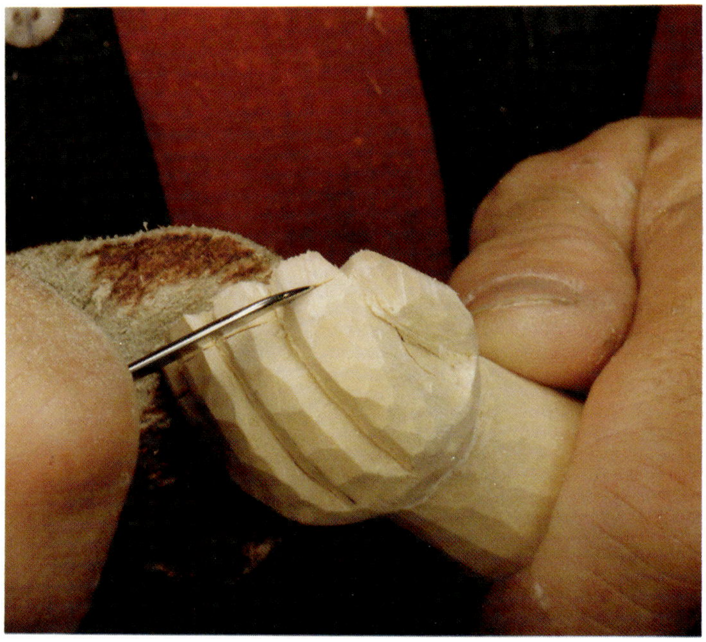

Score a line for each fingernail. We will paint Ruby's nails later to make them stand out.

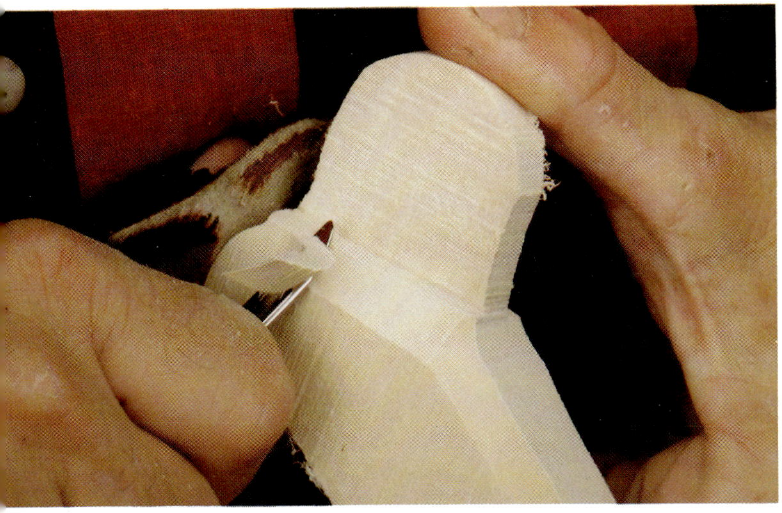

You will need a sharp knife to work on the shoes as you will be rounding across the vertically running grain. Begin rounding the sharp edges of the shoe.

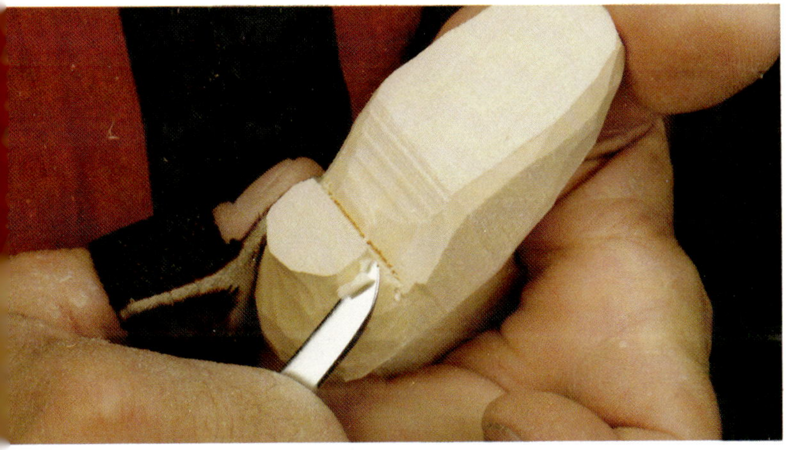

Carve down the heel a bit to create a high heel. Not a stiletto heel mind you, just a high one. With the grain running up and down, this is easy to do. If you were trying to fashion this heel across the grain, you would soon end up with a broken heel.

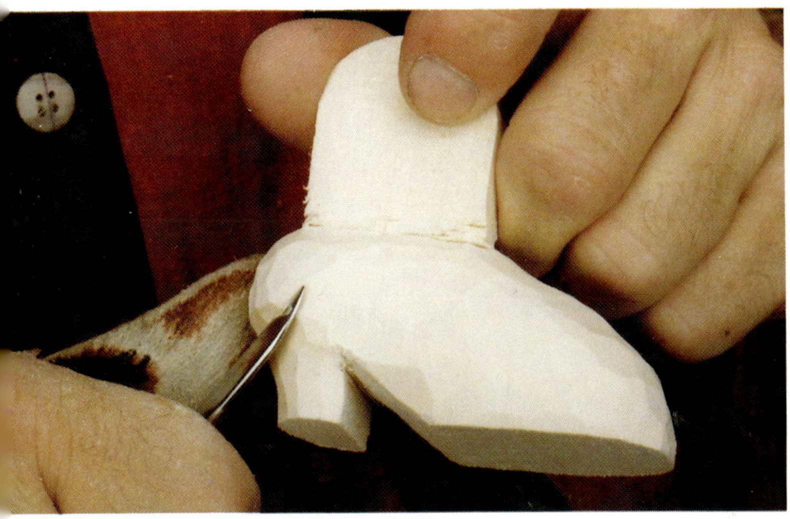

Continue rounding the shoe like this.

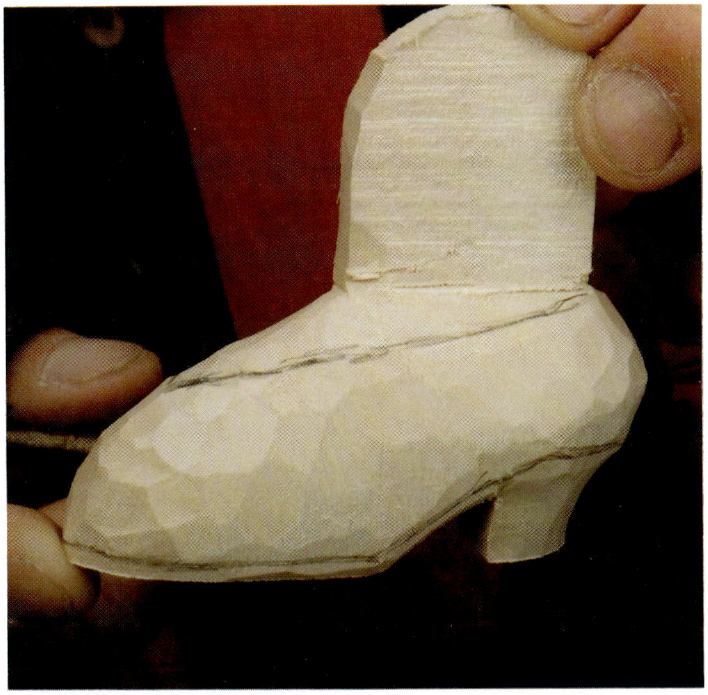

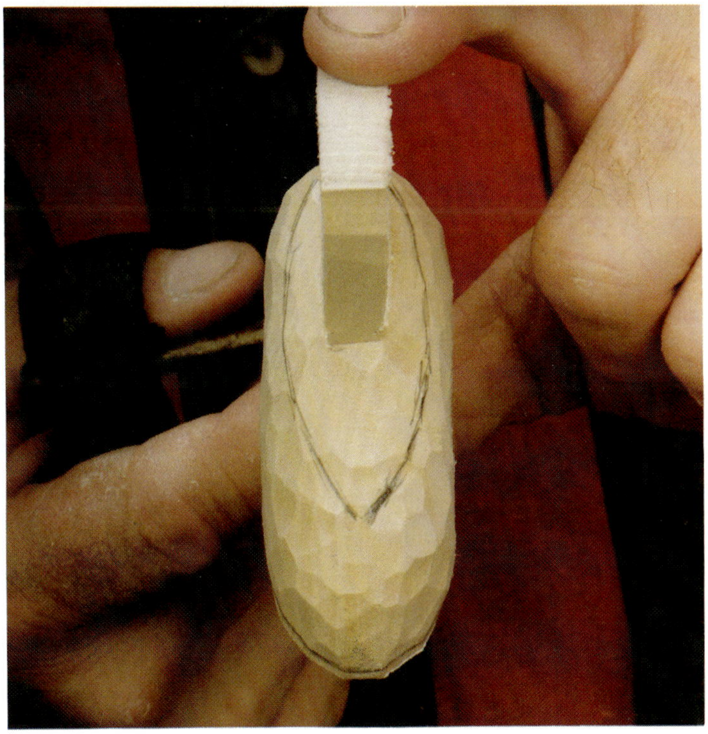

Draw in the outlines of the sole and top of the shoe. Once done, you can say you put your heart and "sole" into this project.

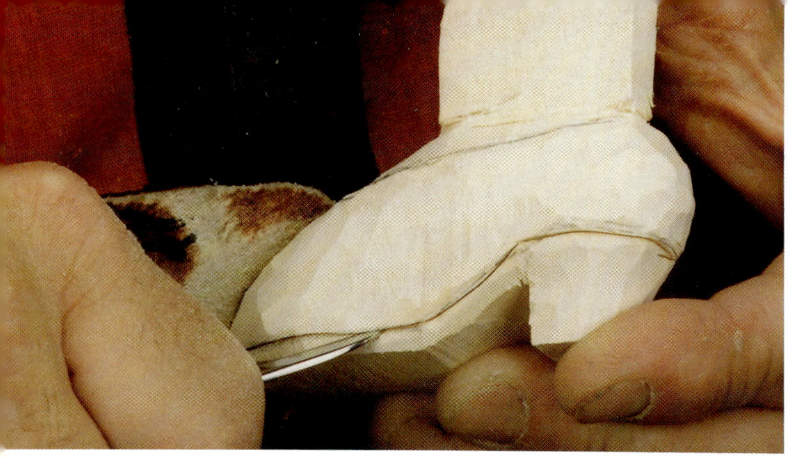

Incise the lines of the shoe. Make the cut deep enough that you will not have trouble making your angled cuts. Angle up to the incised line at the top of the sole. Be careful here, it would be very easy to cut off the sole during this process.

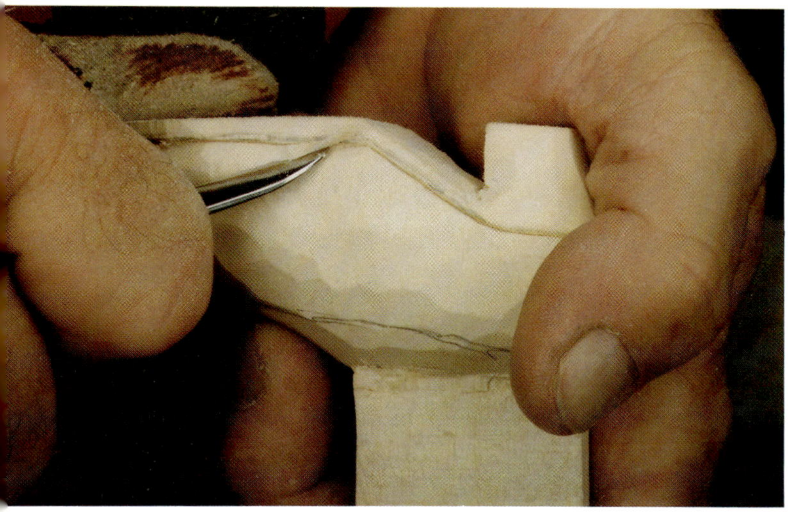

Make an angled cut in to the top of the incised line of the sole as well. This helps give the shoe depth and definition.

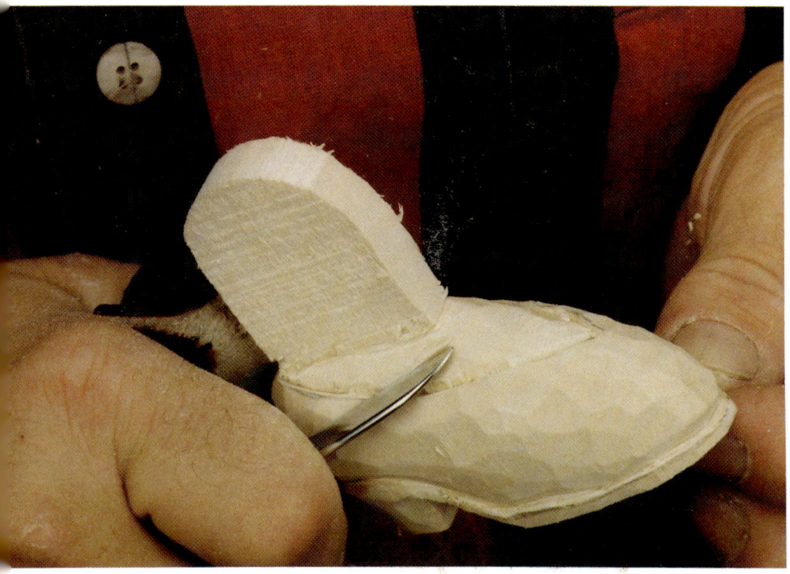

Reduce the top of the foot down below the level of the top of the shoe, working down to the incised line at the shoe.

To carve the wings, first draw in the pattern for the upper feathers.

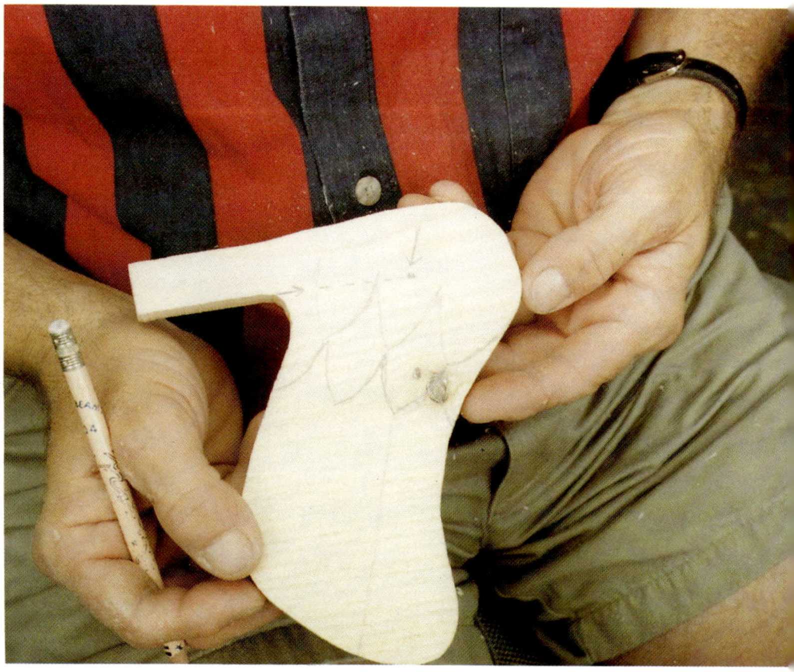

Next, place a single dot half way out from the lower edge of the wing tenon as shown by the dotted line.

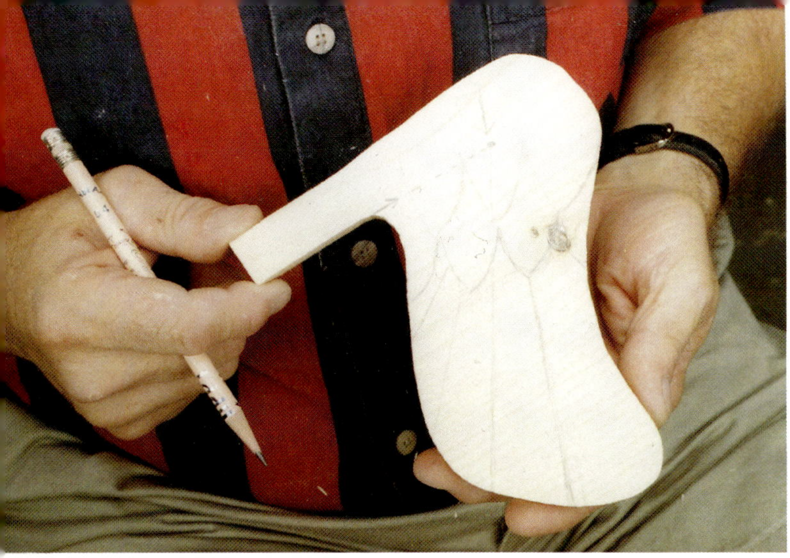

The lines of the wings long lower feathers all radiate out from this single point.

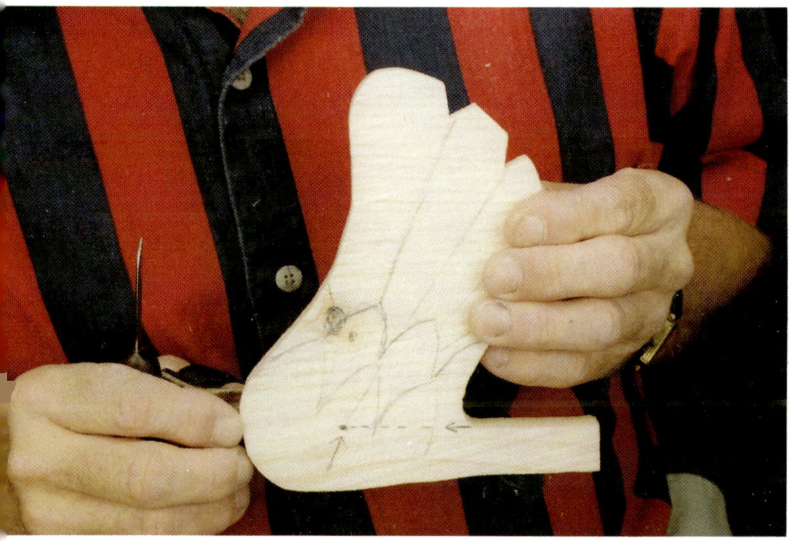

Notch the ends of the long feathers on the bandsaw.

Round off the edges of the wings, front and back. This also tapers the edges of the wings and makes them appear thinner.

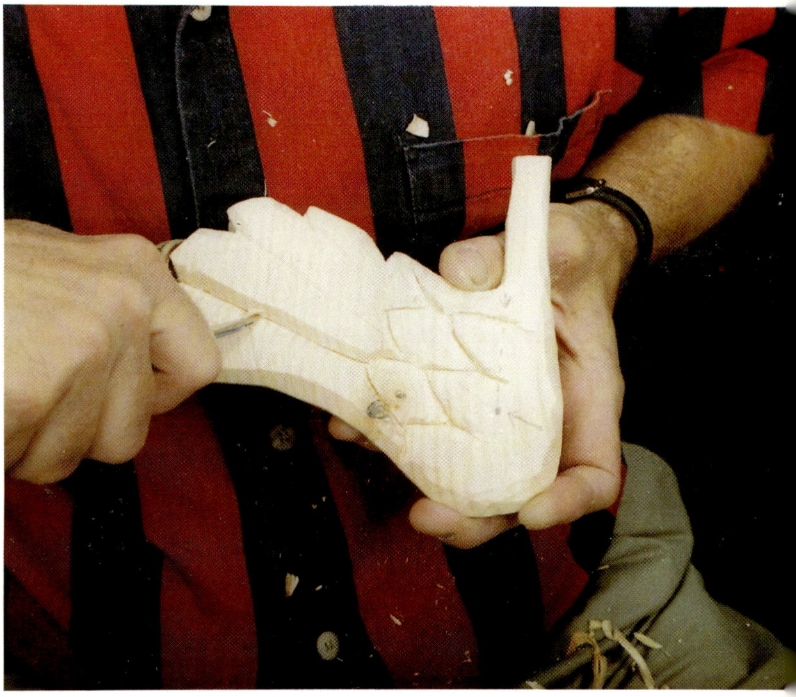

Incise all of the lines on the wing. This only needs to be done along the exposed outer surfaces of the wings. Make a V cut into the incised lines to define the feathers.

Round off the edges of the feathers. Taking the edge off will give the feathers a thinner and more rounded look. Also make sure all of the saw marks are removed at this stage. On the upper feathers, add the long central bone of the feather for detail.

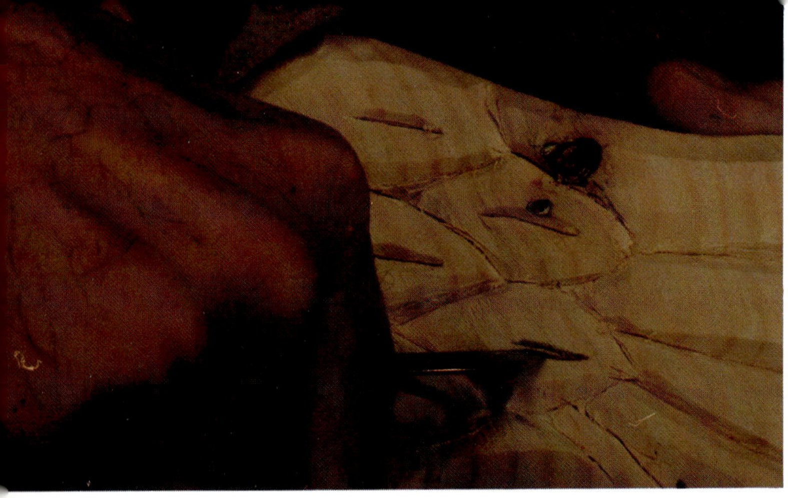

Incise and V cut the lines of each bone in place.

The finished wing.

Hold the arm up against the shoulder. Line the arm up with the center of the head. Draw a line around the arm.

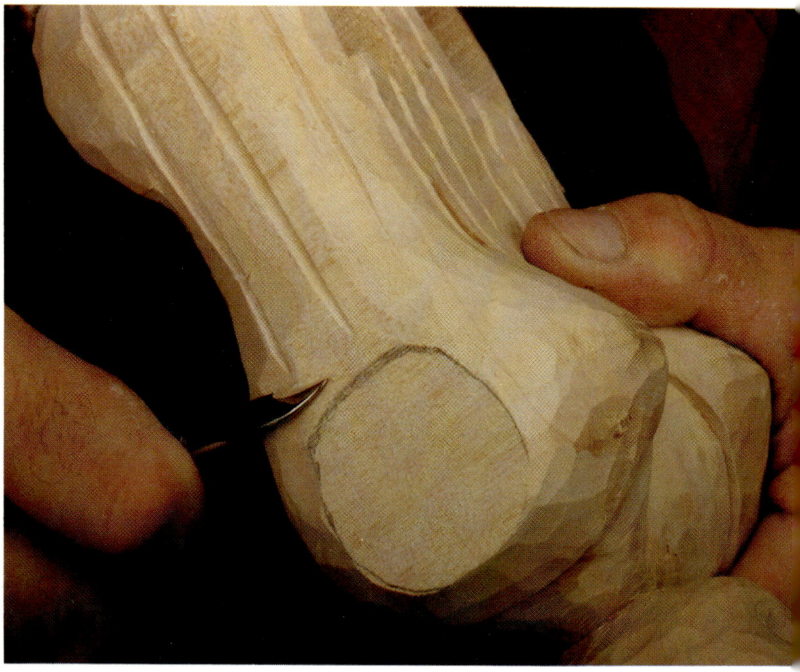

Round the shoulder and the side of the body up to the pencil line to give the body a finished look.

Now it is time to peg the arms and legs together, using a 1/4" dowel and a 7/32" drill bit. This way the dowel is slightly larger than the hole, giving a little resistance and allowing arms and legs to be positioned. Beginning with the upper arm, drill the hole for the peg. Then insert the lower arm into the upper arm. Mark the position for the hole on the lower arm's tenon with an awl or nail.

Drill the peg hole into the tenon. Once the hole is drilled, lay the arm on a block. Line up the holes and carefully drive in the peg. Support the area directly beneath the hole to keep from splitting the piece.

Carefully driving the peg into the arm holes.

Trim away the ends of the peg sticking out on either side of the arm and you are done.

If you notch the tenon for the back of the leg (making sure the tenon does not extend all the way to the back of the leg), the leg will bend a little farther once it is pegged together.

Switching over to a 1/4" bit, matching the size of the dowel, we now drill in the holes for the pegs at the hips and the feet. This allows for more freedom of movement at these joints and keeps from splitting the narrow tenon at the foot. The hole in the center of the hip should be an inch up from the bottom of the hip.

To get the leg correctly positioned to the hips, when bent, the back of the tenon should be flush with the bottom of the hip. That way Ruby will sit well and these figures are best shown seated. Also check to make sure that the leg will fully rotate into a standing position before drilling the hole for the peg.

To match the position of the hole on the other side of the body, draw a line across the front and underneath. The intersection of these two lines roughly matches the location for the peg hole on the opposite hip.

Here is the proper seated posture. The body leans forward a bit to compensate for the weight of the wings we are about to attach.

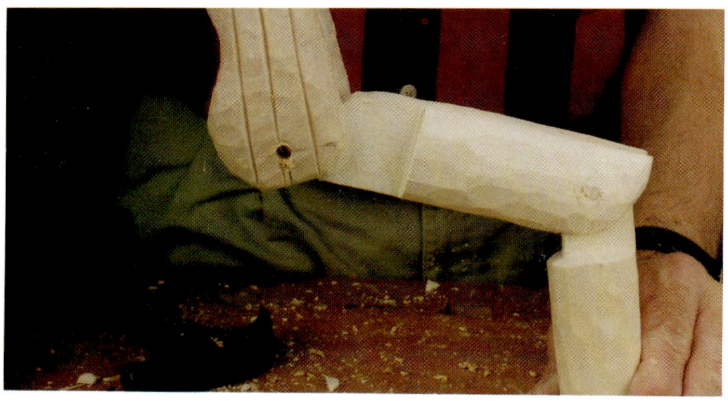

The tenon at the top of the hip is rounded on the leading edge so that Ruby will bend properly. The joint at the knee is also rounded in the back so the lower leg will bend well in the opposite direction.

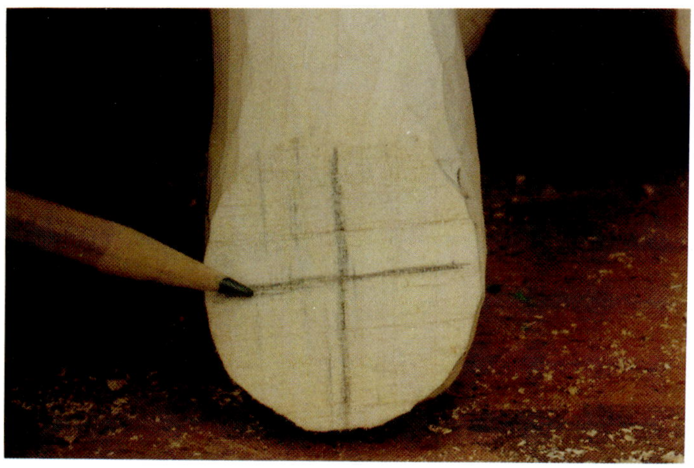

To center the arm properly on the shoulder, locate the center of the joint in pencil.

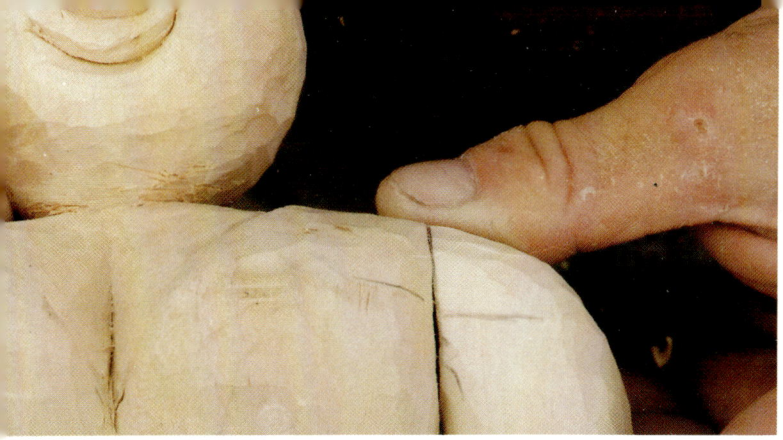

Before drilling, draw a front guide line onto the body to use as a visual aid to keep the bit aligned as you drill.

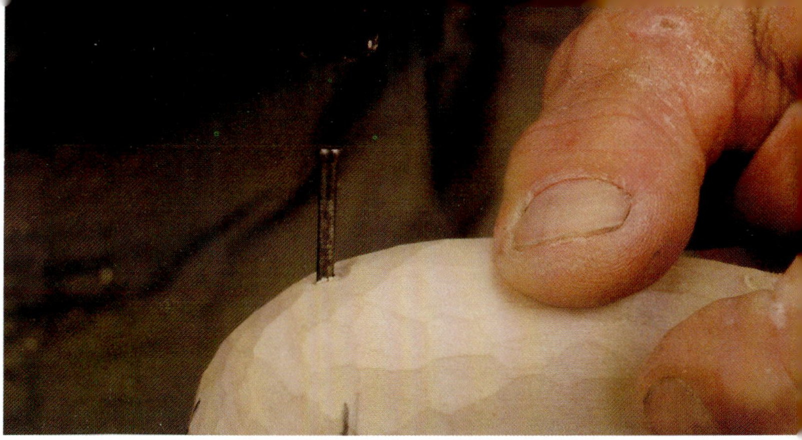

Drive the finishing nail into place.

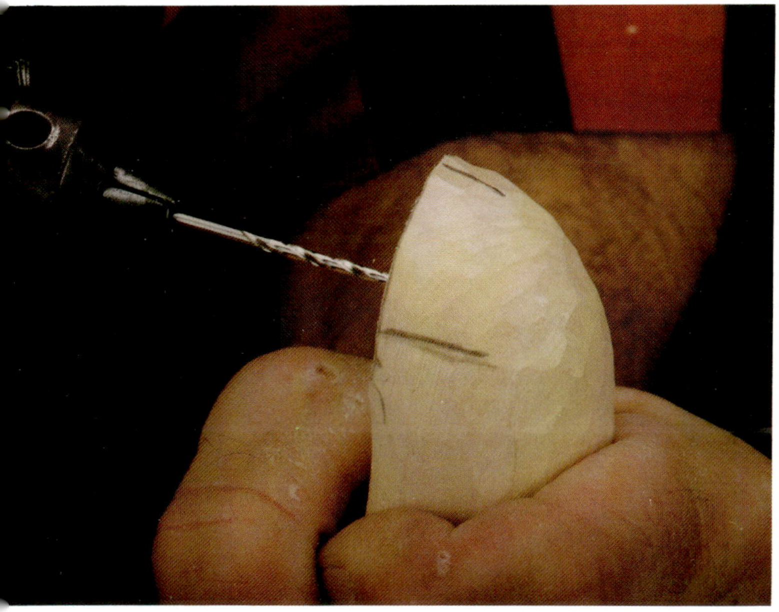

Switch to a very small 3/32" drill bit, which is smaller than the finishing nail that will attach the upper arm. Align the bit with the guidelines on the upper arm joint and with guide marks along the top and side of the arm. Drill the hole straight through. A nail is used instead of a peg at the shoulder because everyone wants to move the arms and the nail withstands this wear and tear better than the peg.

Use a nail set to drive the nail head below the outer surface of the arm. Don't worry about the hole, we'll fill it with spackle later.

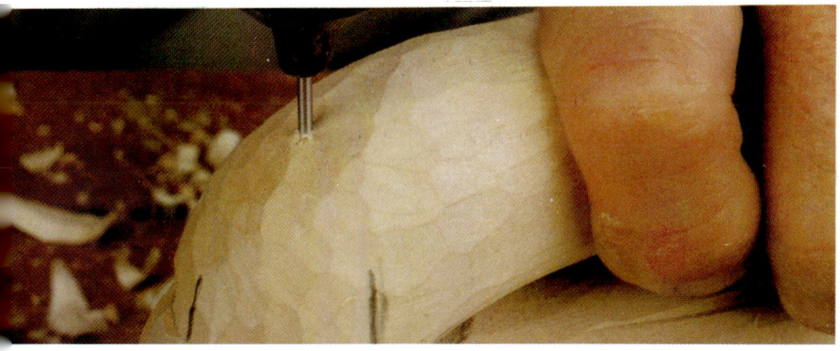

Once the hole in the upper arm is drilled, place the arm against the shoulder and drill on into the body.

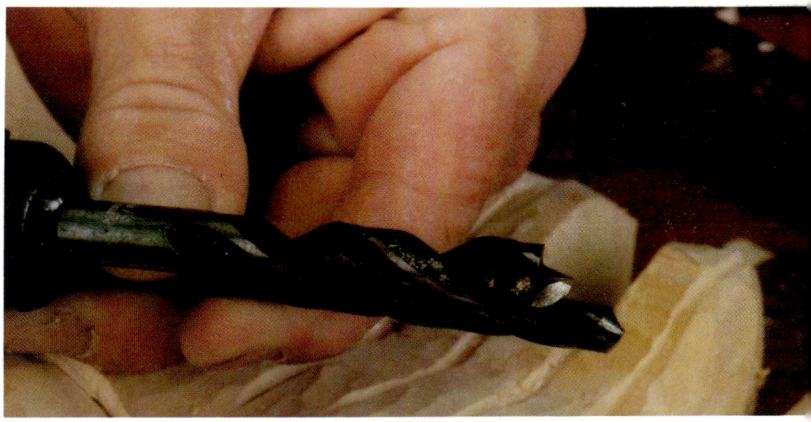

Moving on to the wings, switch to a 3/8" sharp brad point drill bit. This bit will not "walk" on you as a regular bit might when making the compound angle needed to insert the wing. The brad point drill bit is shown mounted in the drill chuck.

Lay the body on its face and hold the wings up to it. See what wing angle looks best to you. Remember, however, you need to miss the nails holding the upper arms in place.

Make sure, when you drill your holes, that they are roughly at the same angle and depth or the wings will appear uneven.

Once the first hole is in place, I put a pencil in the hole to help me match the angle of the hole for the other wing.

Now carve down the wing tenon to fit tightly into the drilled hole and insert the wing.

I use Dap Kwik Seal to create texture for the hair. Apply it all over the top of the head, covering the wood area. This product will dry hard and can be painted over. We didn't carve ears on this figure because her hair covers the ears.

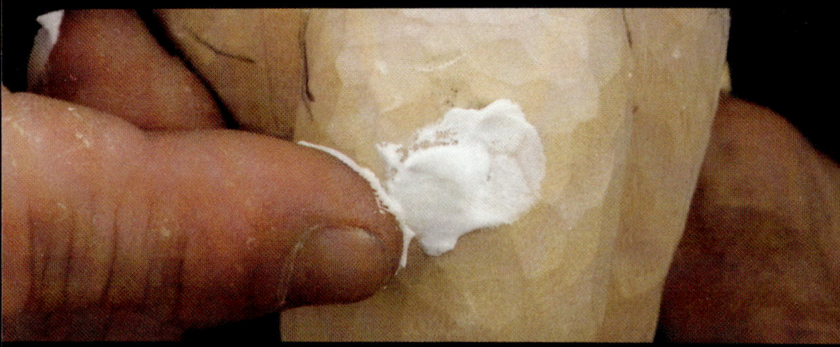

Take a little spackling compound and fill the nail holes. Once dried, we will be able to sand this smooth. Also use the spackle to fill any cracks you might find.

Ruby is completed and ready for paint.

Carving Angelene, the Angel Whirligig

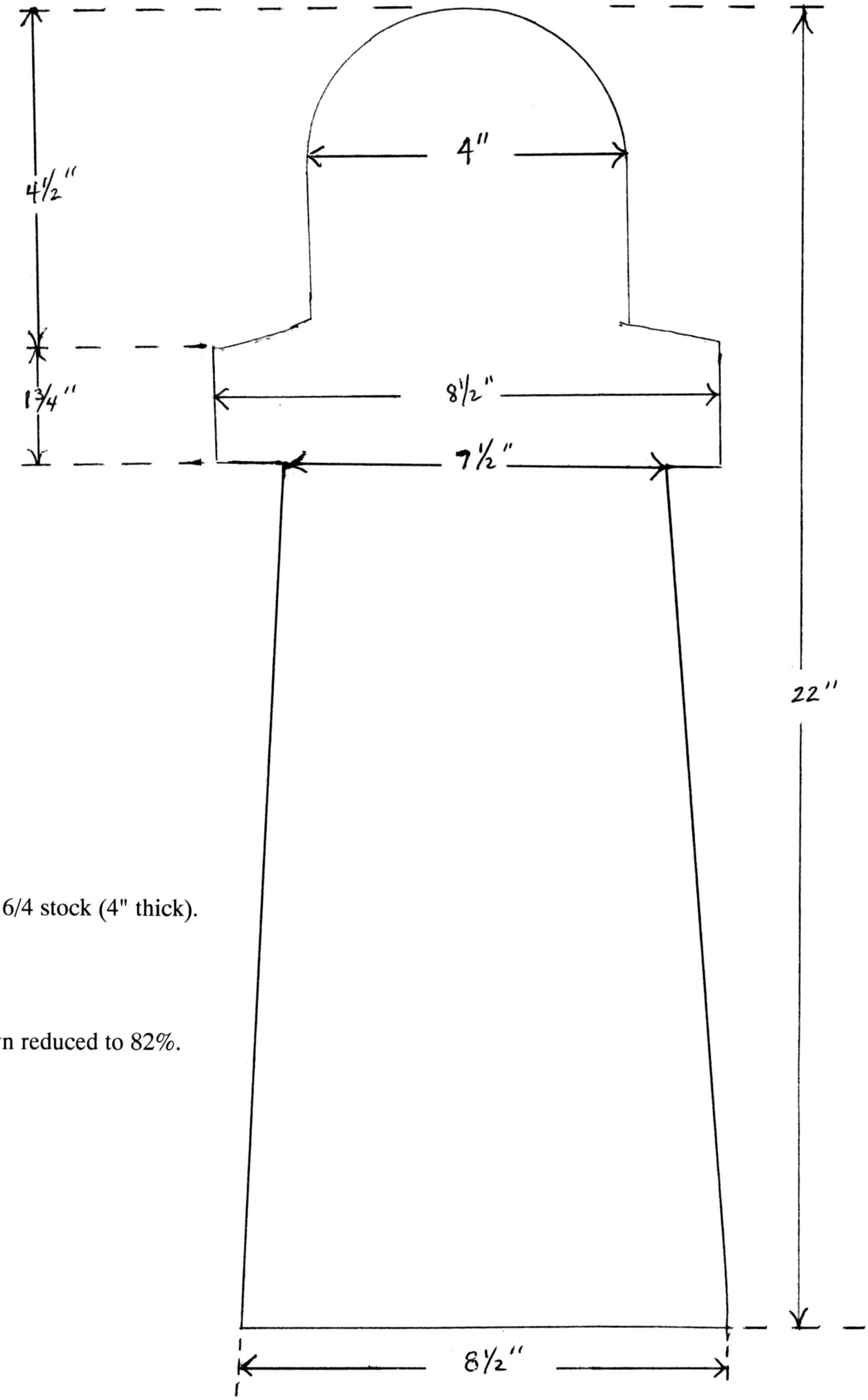

"Angelene" 16/4 stock (4" thick).

Pattern shown reduced to 82%.

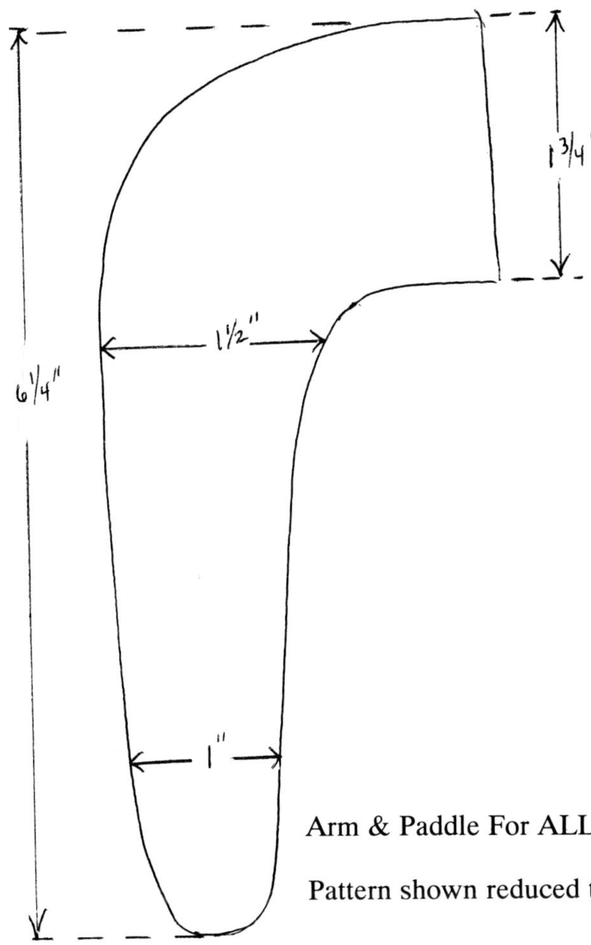

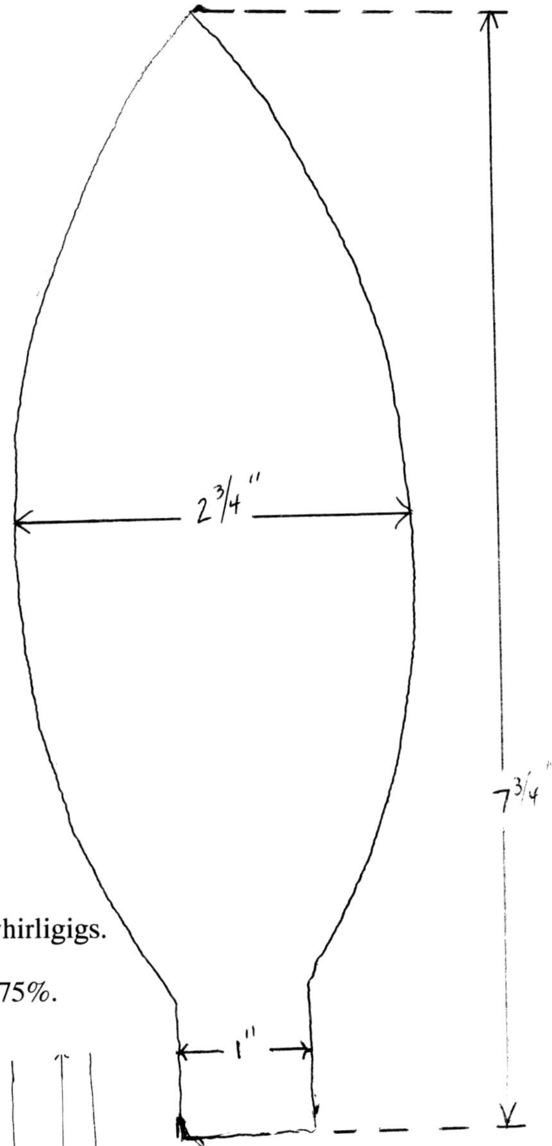

Arm & Paddle For ALL whirligigs.

Pattern shown reduced to 75%.

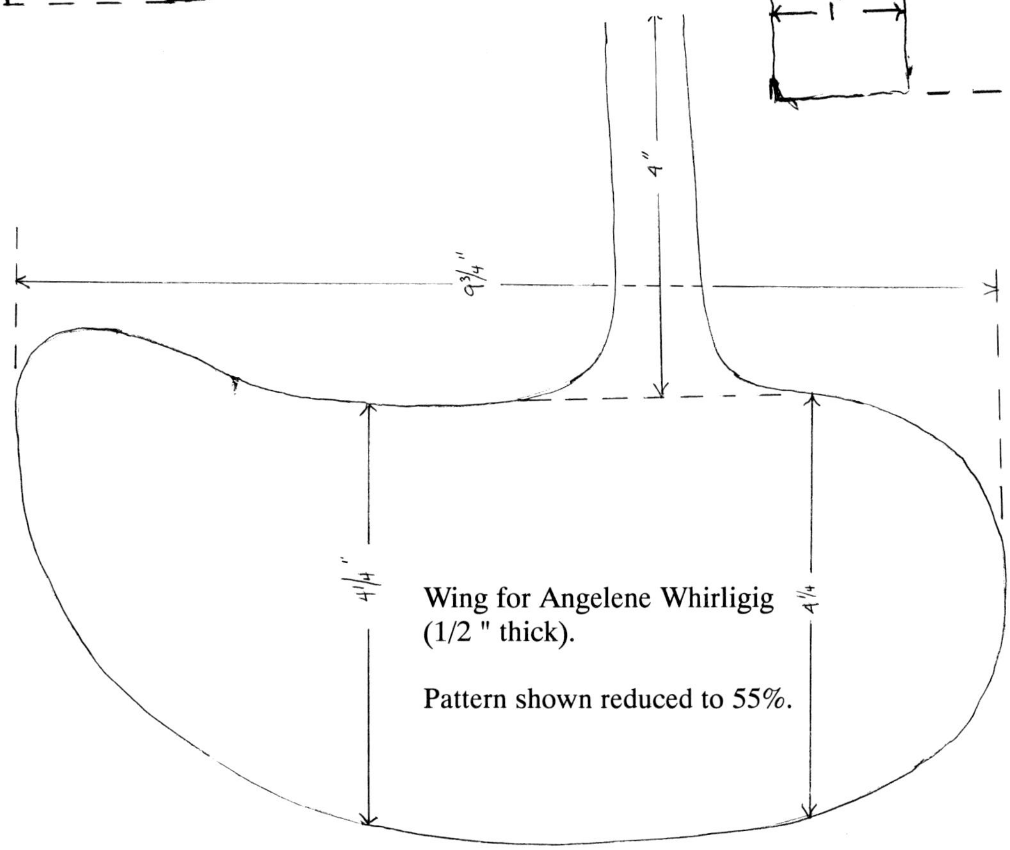

Wing for Angelene Whirligig (1/2 " thick).

Pattern shown reduced to 55%.

Use twelve-quarter (3") thick lumber for your whirligig angel. Angelene measures 8 1/2" wide across the shoulders. If this thickness cannot be obtained from a single piece of lumber, you can always glue up stock to this thickness. I did. Angelene also measures 22" long. While the wood is still square, the first thing to do is drill the hole for the dowel that will hold the rotating arms. This hole must be drilled straight through the wood so that the dowel will pass straight through easily.

To line up the drill, find the center on both sides of the lumber. First, take one of the rough cut arms and mark the outer edges of the arm. Then take a square and draw diagonals. Where the lines intersect will be the center, the location the drill needs to pass through on either side of the whirligig. You may draw centerlines along the front face and top of the block. These lines act as guides when you "eyeball" the drill hole through the block. On the other hand, you may use a drill press (if you have one) to accomplish the same task with more precision.

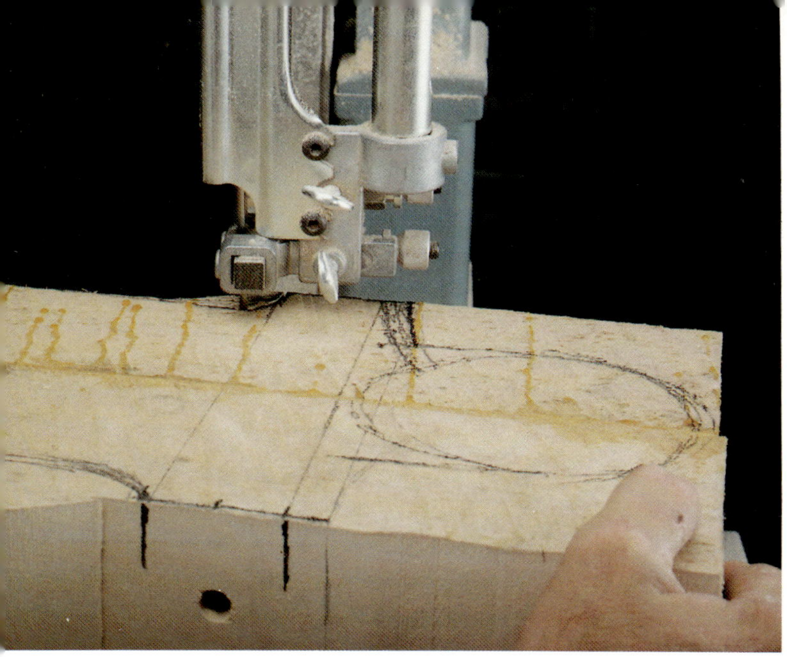

Cut out the whirligig's front pattern.

Cut out the wing and split it in half as before to create two wings of the proper thickness.

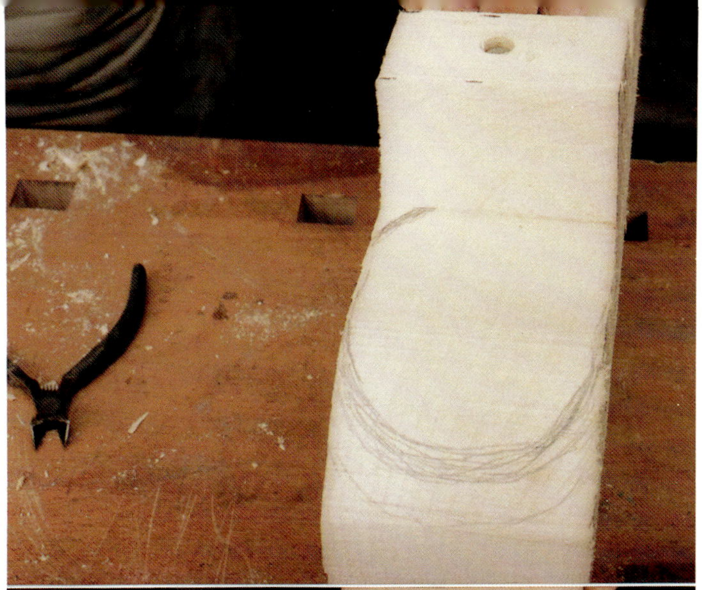

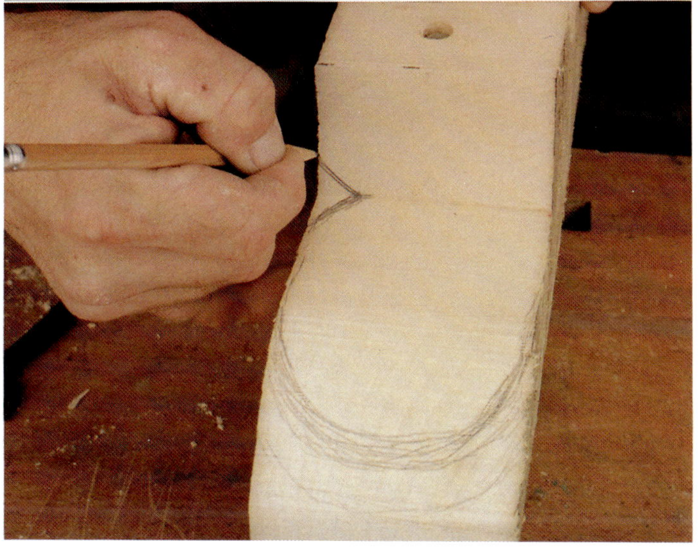

Here are the profile guidelines for the head and neck. Cut along these guides with the bandsaw.

The head is now roughed in.

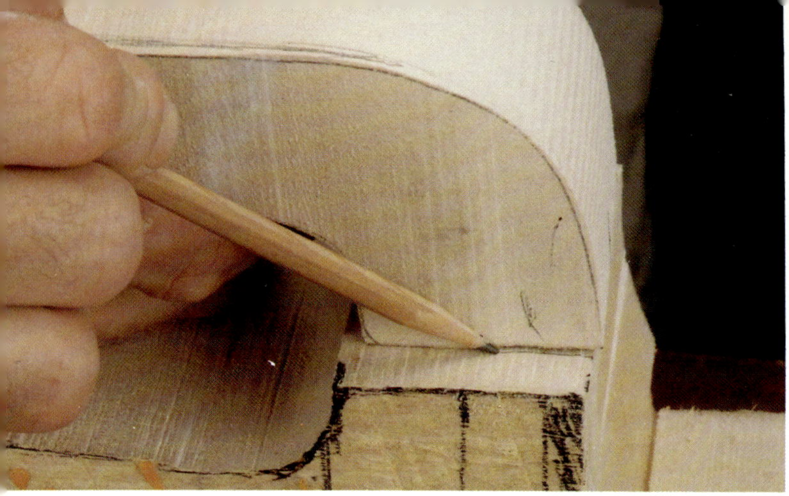

Hold the roughed out arm in place and mark the outer edges along the shoulder joint so that you don't reduce the size of the shoulder too much.

Draw in the boundaries of the hair line. This will keep you from removing too much wood and ending up with a bald angel. Work down the areas around the hairline.

Using a #8 fishtail gouge, round off the form. Because this gouge takes off a lot of wood at a time, it is necessary to clamp the piece down in order to avoid getting hurt.

Continue rounding the sides with the #8 fishtail gouge.

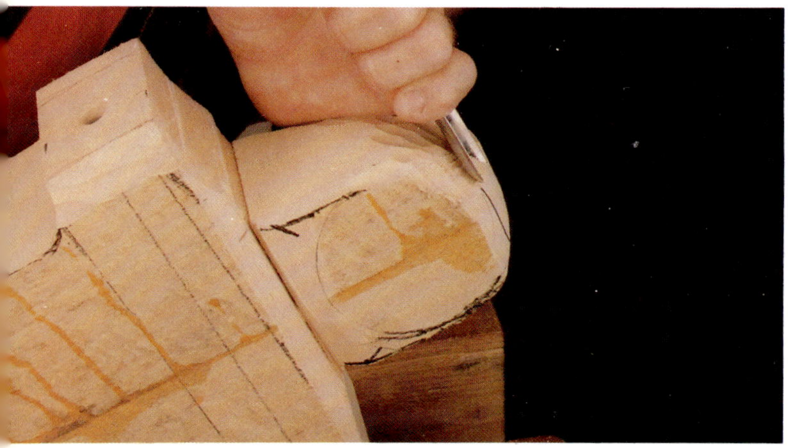

Rounding the head. You have to use a lot of pressure to do this and need to have the piece securely clamped to avoid injury.

Use the bent gouge along the curve of the shoulders. It rounds a corner very well.

Continuing to round the head, making sure to leave plenty of wood for the hair.

Rounding the front of the body. Whirligigs were left very plain, so we don't have to worry about this angel's bust line.

This is how the hair will fall down the angel's back.

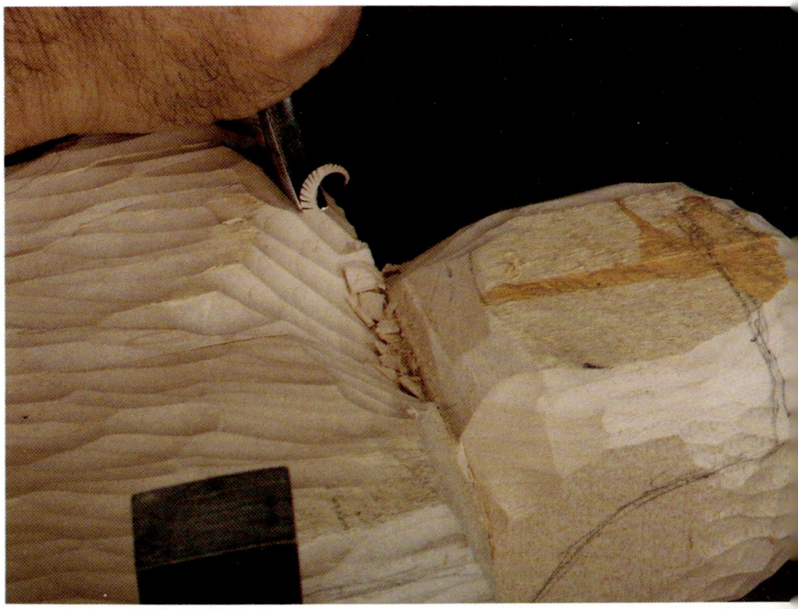

The back of the angel is rounded down. Draw in the pattern lines for her hair again.

Round the angle of the chest down into the neck.

Continuing to round down into the neck with a #2 flat chisel. The flat chisel takes off less wood at a time and is good for close work.

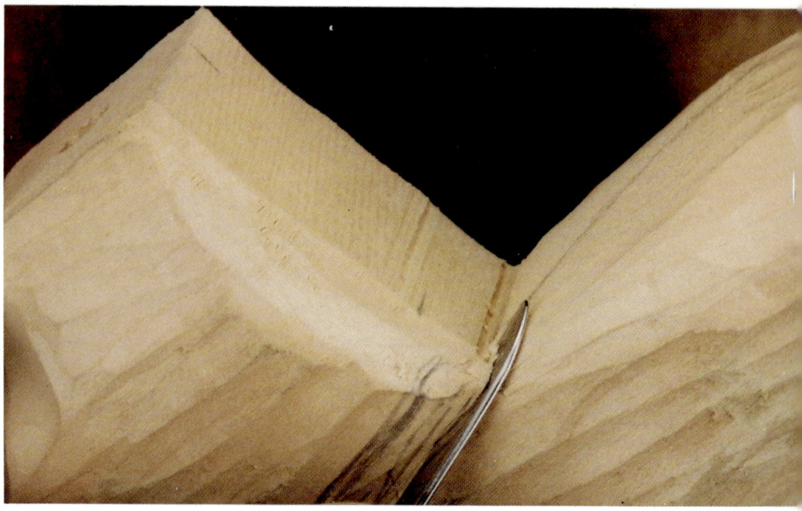

Use the bench knife to finish rounding the head in areas the chisel could not easily reach.

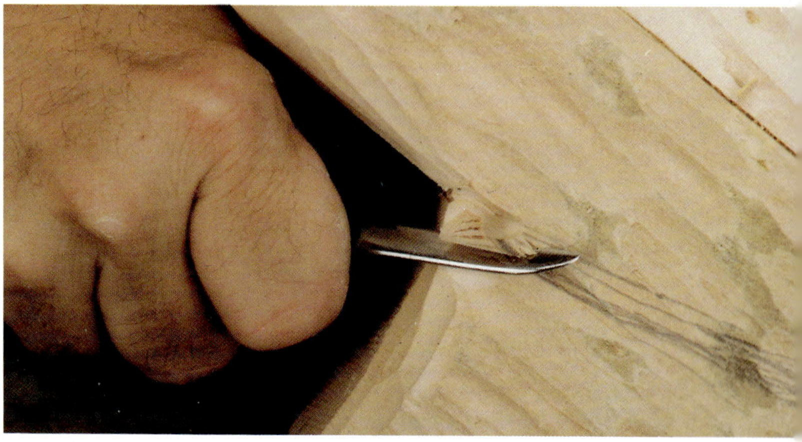

Make a stop cut along the hair line where the hair intersects with the shoulder. Cut back to the hair line from the shoulder and remove excess wood, raising the hair above the new shoulder level.

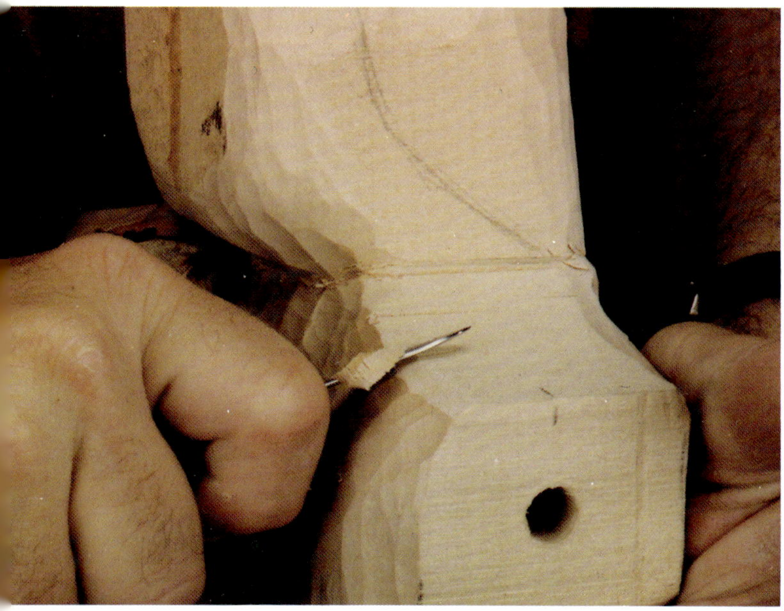

Round the shoulders with the bench knife as well.

Incise the line of the hair down the angel's back, cutting straight in along the hair line. Cut in at an angle from the body into that stop cut to separate the hair from the back.

Cut in just a little at the intersection of the shoulder and the hair, exposing a little more hair. However, don't cut in too much or the shoulder will appear narrower at the neck than at the attachment between the shoulder and the upper arm.

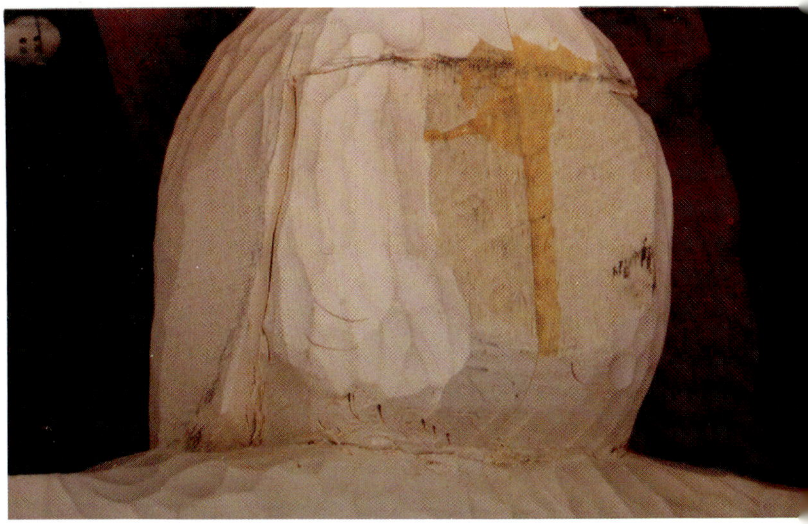

Begin rounding the bottom of the face, working back to the incised hair line.

By reducing the shoulder a little at the hair line, the hair now nicely, smoothly flows over the shoulder and down the back.

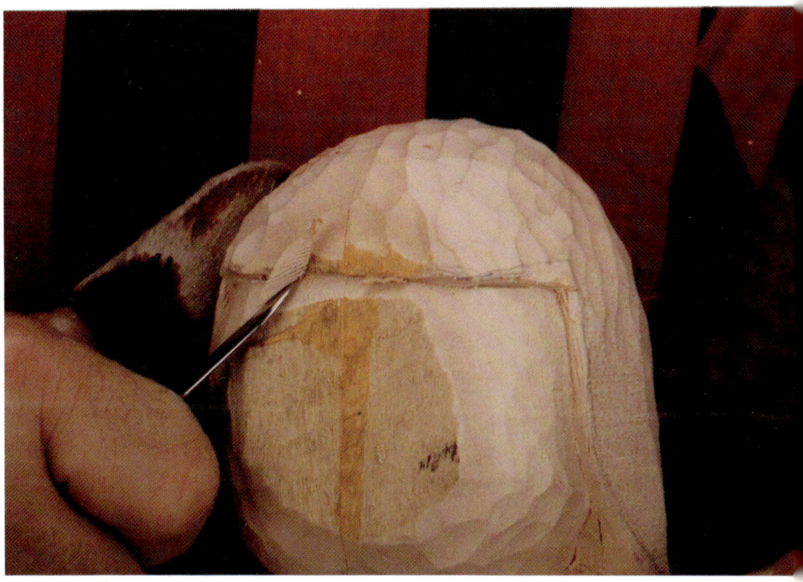

Continuing to round down the head.

Incise the hair line around the front of the head.

Add the lines for the eyebrows and nose as before.

Incise the lines and make angled cuts from the face down to the incised lines as you did with Ruby.

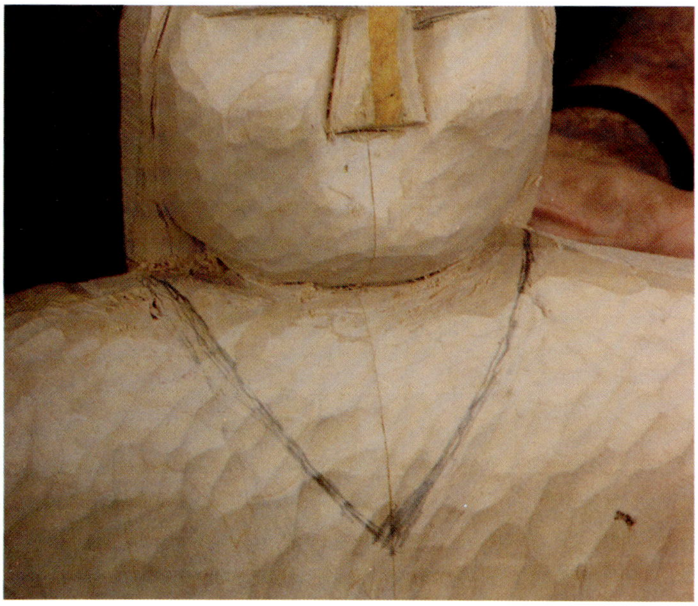

Round down the lower jaw and neck line, leaving the cheek bones high and pronounced. Draw in the V neck collar.

Here is the arm pattern. Follow this pattern to cut out the blank on the bandsaw.

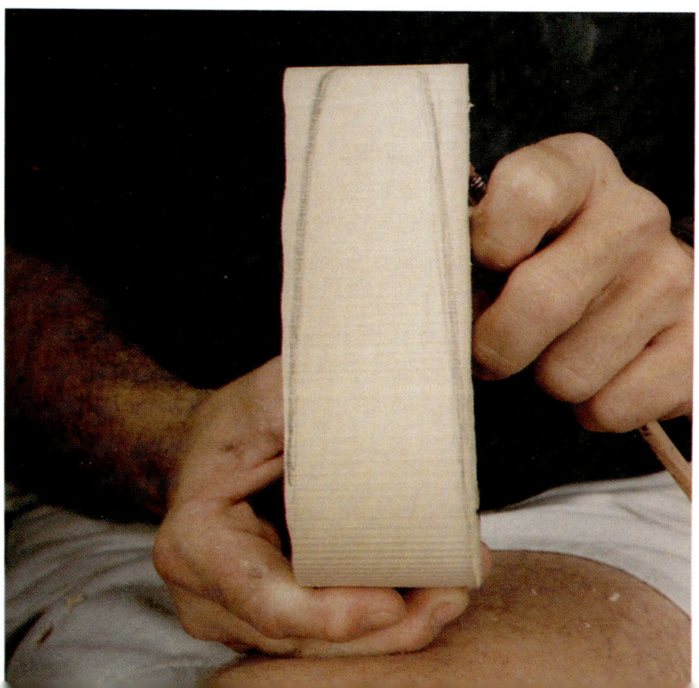

Round down the arm with the bench knife, tapering and refining the shape as you go. Make sure to remove all of the saw marks. Notice that the top of the arm (where it attaches to the body) is left alone. It is already square and needs no additional work.

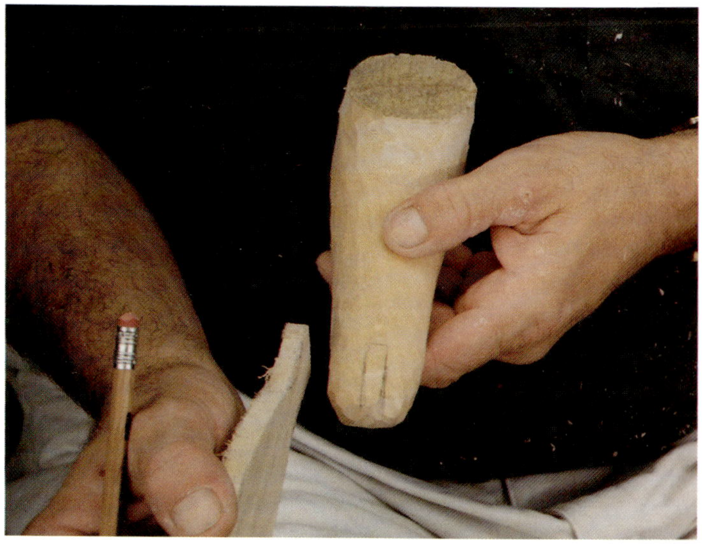

The arm is rounded. Use the roughed out paddle tenon to pattern the slot at the end of the arm into which that tenon will fit. (The paddle is roughly 3/8" thick.) When cutting out the slot, make sure to cut inside the pattern lines. This will ensure a tight fit when the paddle tenon is inserted.

The slot was cut on the bandsaw and the paddle fit is tight.

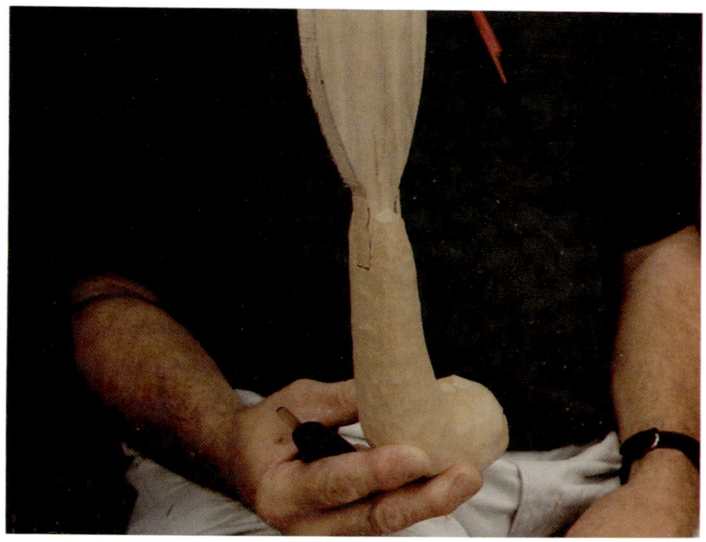

Round the paddle, with the exception of the tenon. Basically, just feather the edge on both sides to make the paddle appear thinner.

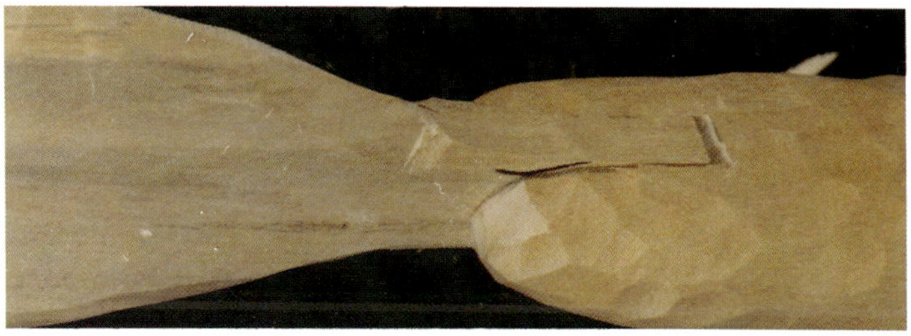

Once the paddle tenon is in place, carve away excess wood until the tenon is flush with the arm.

Moving on to the wing ... draw in the dot from which all your feather lines will radiate. The dot is located about an inch from the inner edge of the wing and is extended out from the center of the tenon.

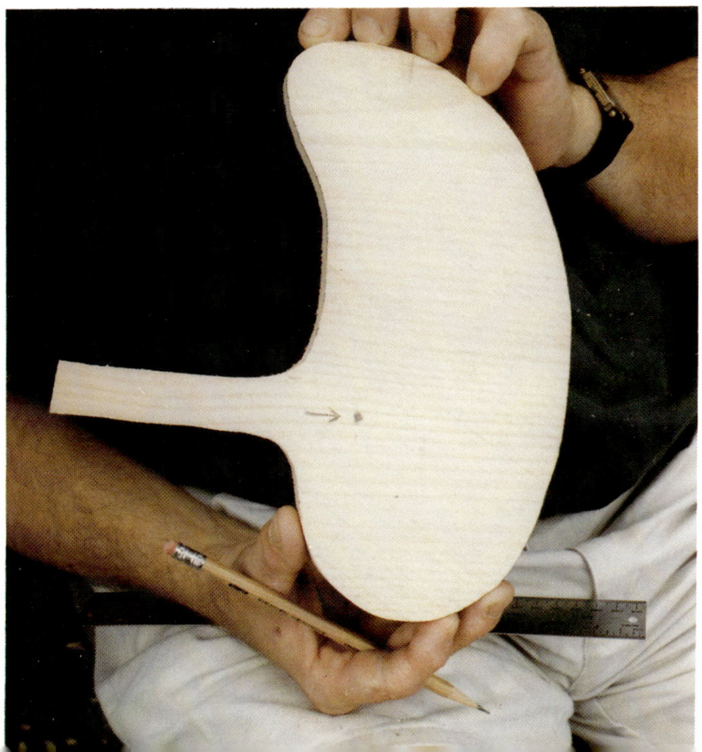

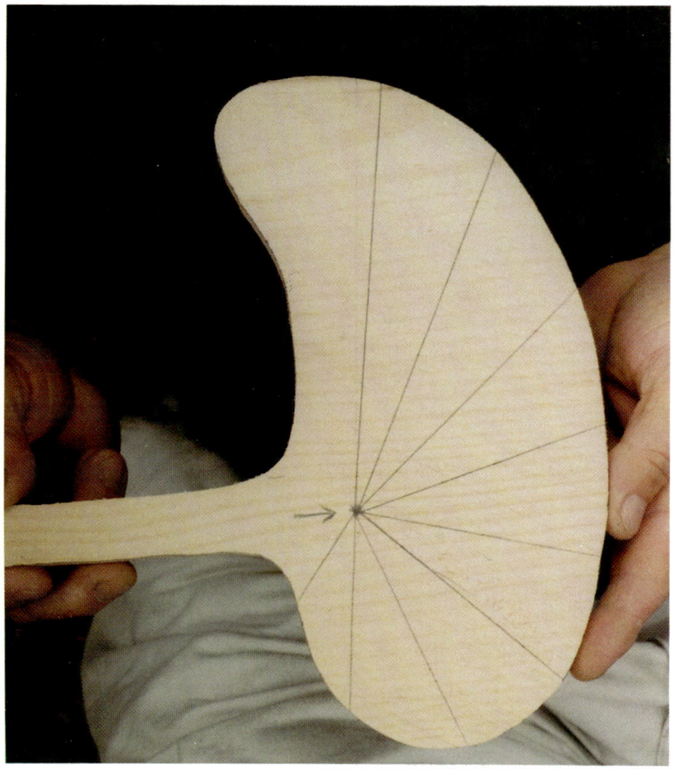

Draw in the lines of your feathers.

Use the bandsaw to cut in notches at the edges of the feathers. These are done free hand. Try to keep them regular and of about the same depth. If you cut the first one deeper or shallower than you intended, just cut the rest to match. Don't panic.

Round the edges of the wings with the bench knife.

The completed wing.

Incise the feather lines and make angled cuts to finish the feathers. Make sure the angled cuts extend outward from the center point. The center point is the most delicate area. Carving away from that point, rather than toward it, will reduce the chances of chipping the wings.

Returning to the face, it is time to carve a smiling mouth with teeth. Draw in the pattern of the mouth and teeth.

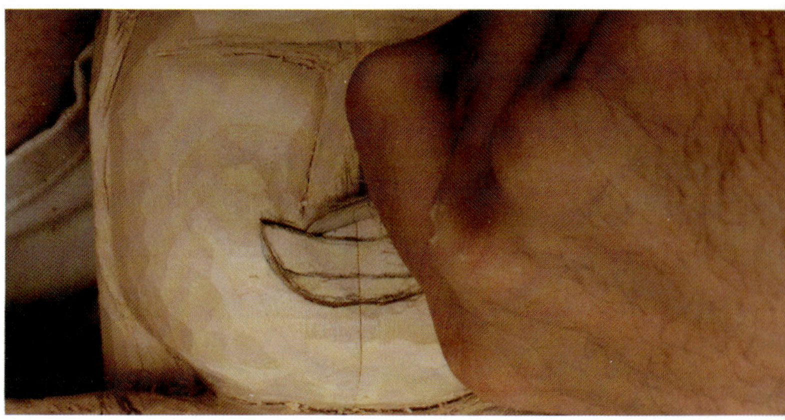

Incise the lines of the mouth and teeth.

Make deep V cuts on either side of the teeth to make them appear round. Also reduce the wood of the teeth down a hair from the edge of the lip. This will recess the teeth back into the mouth a bit.

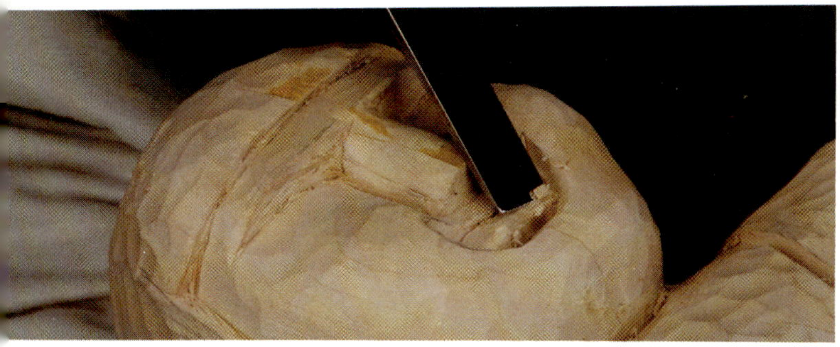

Use a #2 flat gouge to reduce the bottom part of the teeth to be level with the top of the teeth. This will keep Angelene from appearing buck-toothed.

The mouth should look like this at this point.

Draw in the lines for the individual teeth.

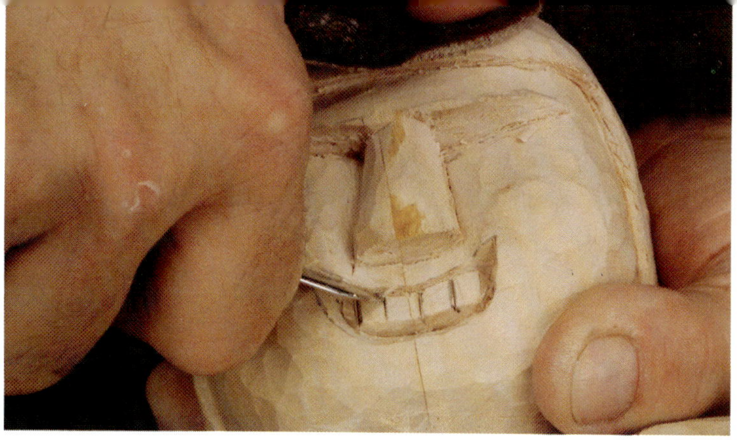

Lightly incise along these lines and make a tiny angled cut along one side of the line to separate each tooth.

Angelene now has a brilliant smile.

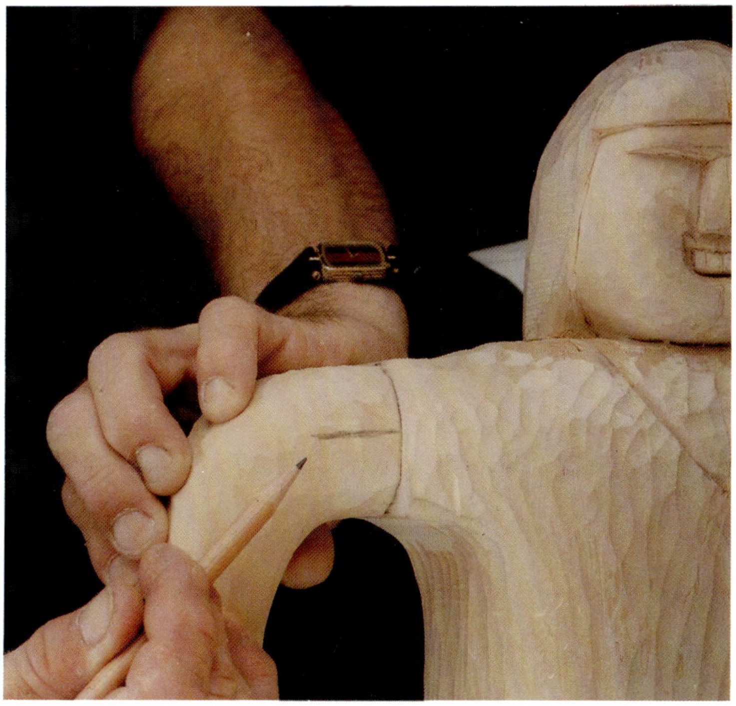

Draw guide lines to follow when drilling the center hole in the arm. The dowel passing through the whirligig will fit into this center hole.

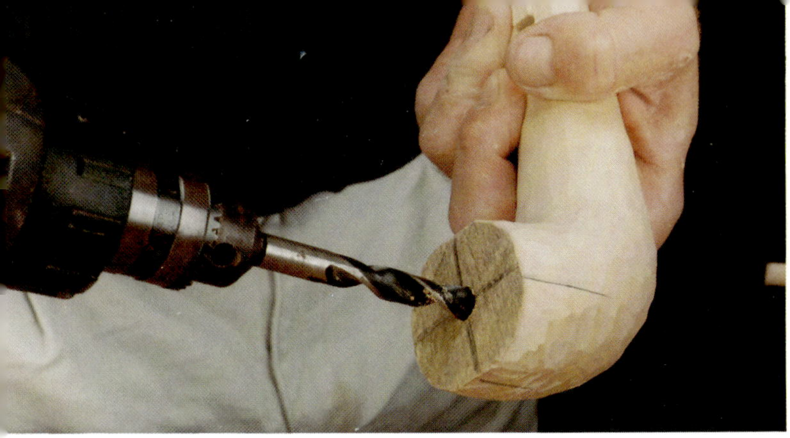

Following your guide lines, use a 3/8" brad point bit to drill the hole for the dowel. The brad point bit is for woodworking and is designed to drill an accurate hole as the point holds the bit in the right position as you drill. If you should happen to drill you hole a little off center, fill the hole with a piece of 3/8" dowel, glue it in place, and redrill when the glue is dried.

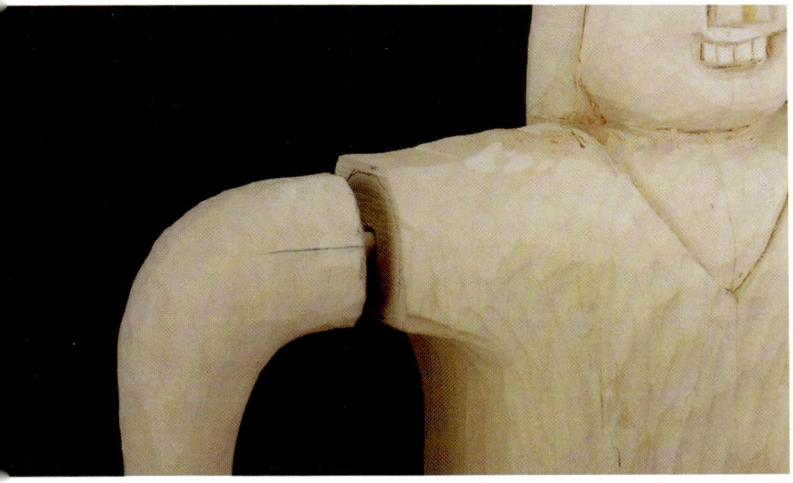

Insert the 3/8" dowel, fit the arm to the dowel, and mark the edge of the arm on the shoulder in pencil prior to rounding down the shoulder to meet the arm. The fit between the arm and shoulder only needs to be good, not perfect. The arm needs a little wiggle room to turn freely.

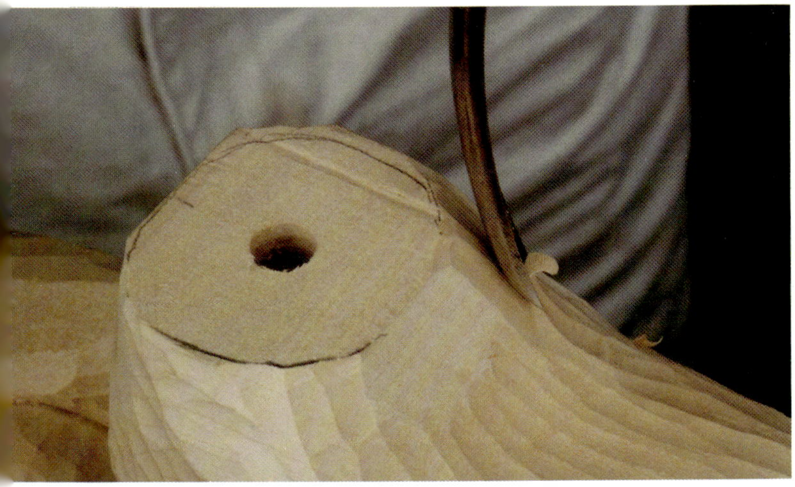

Round the shoulder down to the guide lines. I use a combination of the bent chisel and the knife to accomplish this. Use whatever tool works best for you in any particular instant.

The arm and shoulder fit together well now.

Use a #8 fishtail gouge to feather out the edges around the hair in back to make it appear as if the hair is raised above the surface of the back.

Round down the edge of the hair in back to remove sharp edges.

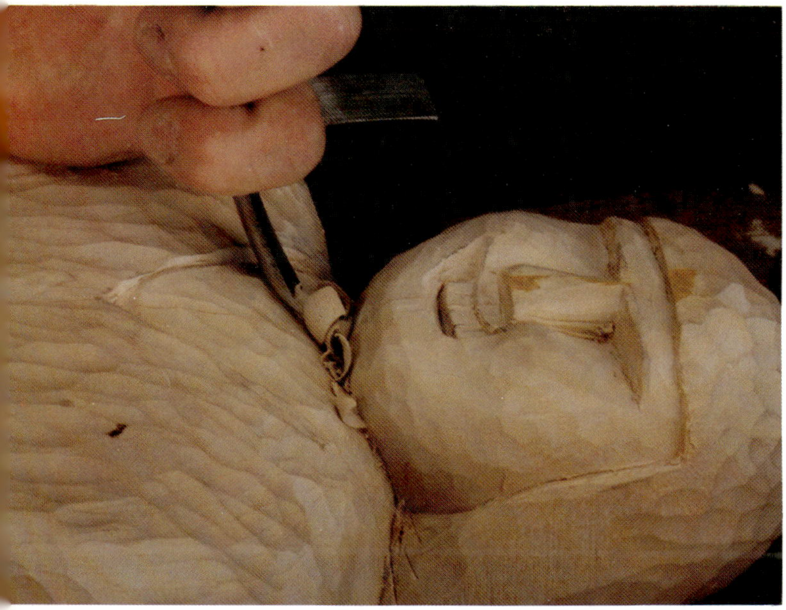

Use the gouge to define the neck line and to lower the neck and exposed upper chest below the level of the dress.

The chest is lowered. Use the #2 gouge now to carefully lower the dress a bit so that it does not appear too thick or to be raised too far above Angelene's body.

Glue the paddle in place. For looks alone, use a 1/4" drill bit to drill through the arm and paddle tenon. A peg will be inserted into the hole to give the appearance that the arm and paddle are pegged together. Here is the guide mark showing the location for the peg.

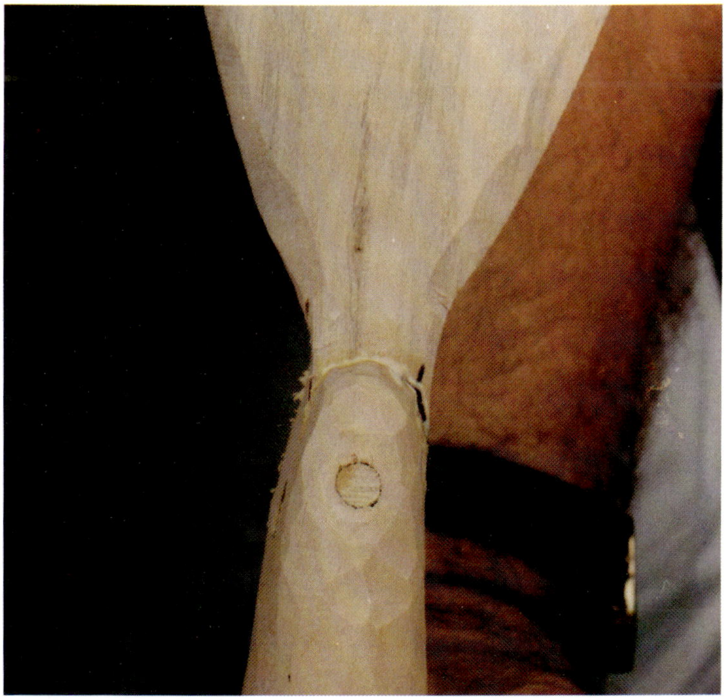

Sharpen the end of the peg as it is the same size as the drilled hole and this will make it easier to insert. Add a little dab of glue and insert the peg. Cut the peg flush with the surface of the arm. The peg is in place.

Locate the wings, preferably outside of the hair line. The most important point is that the wings must be located below the hole the dowel passes through. However, the wings need to be high enough to be seen over the top of the head when seen from the front. Otherwise, you wouldn't know Angelene was an angel.

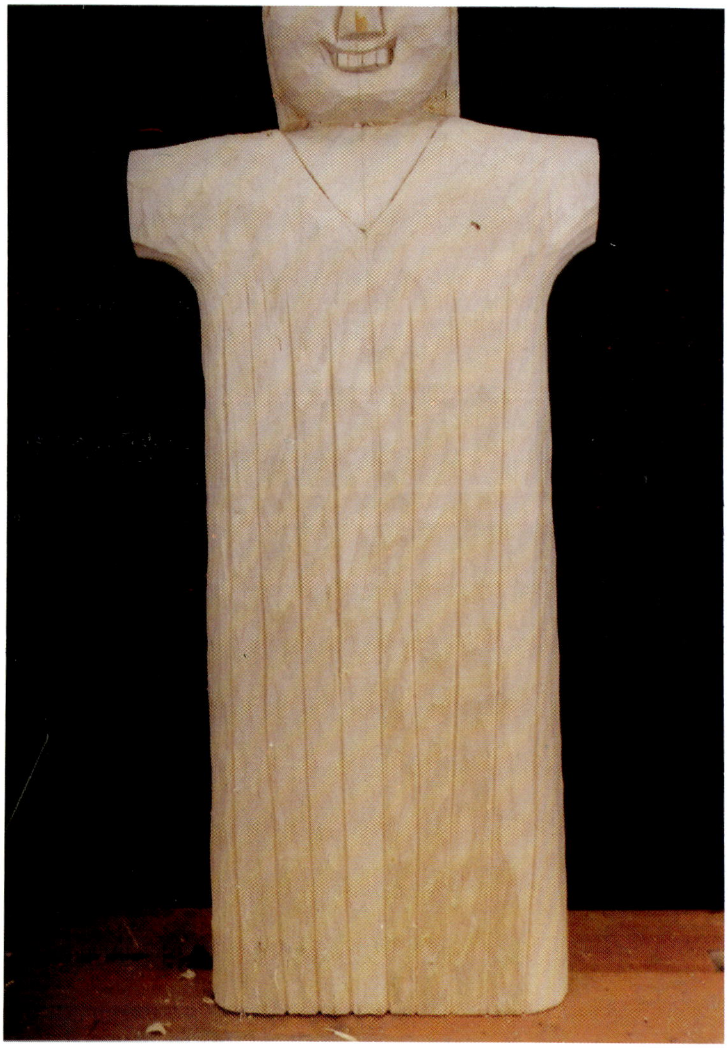

Use a small V gouge to cut folds into the gown. This is pure free-hand work.

The tenon has been left large and will be carved to fit the hole after it has been drilled. You need the tenon to be as large as possible to avoid wing breakage. Use a 1/2" bit to drill the holes for the wings. While the wings will be straight vertically, I like to cant them to the sides a bit. Use the same steps as before to match the angle of the wings. Make certain, however, that you don't angle the wings out so far that they interfere with the turning paddles at the ends of the arms.

Reduce the size of the tenon just enough so that it can be forced snugly into the hole. Glue the wings in place.

Once the arms and wings are attached, Angelene is ready for painting. When attaching the arms, make sure they are exactly opposite each other in position (arm up and arm down) so that they will balance and turn easily in the wind. Angelene is ready to paint, using whatever color combinations please you. We will cover my painting techniques by painting Ruby.

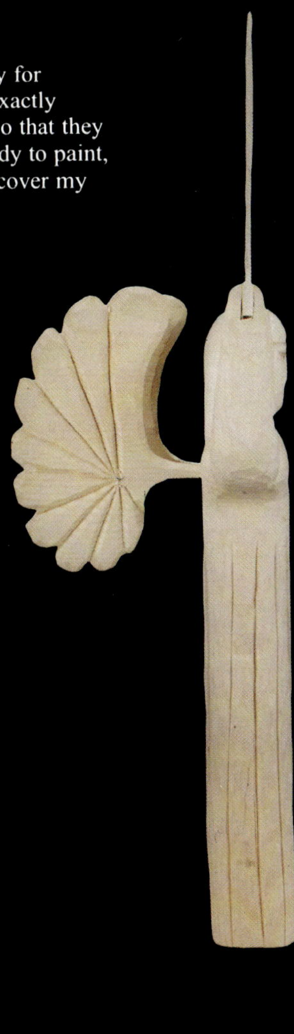

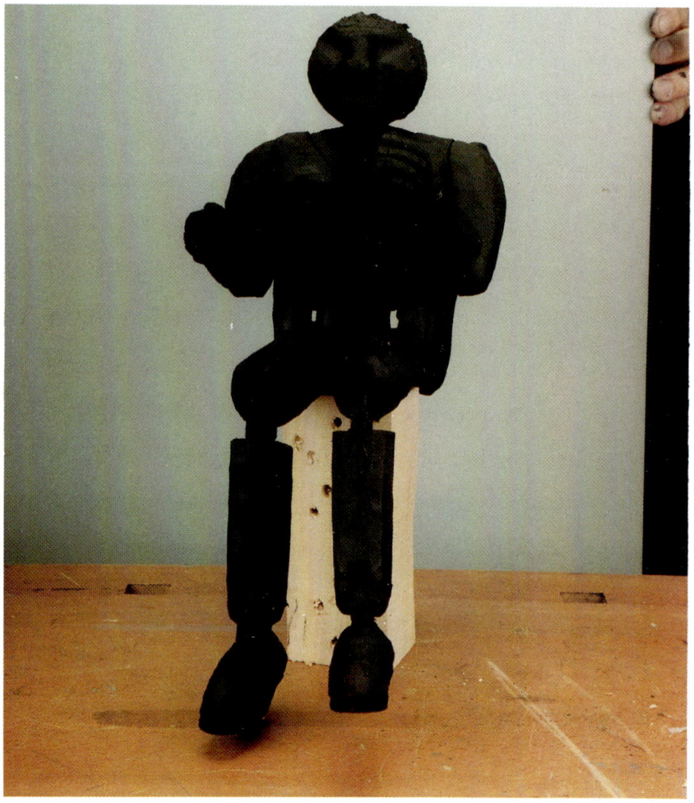

Presented here are the steps for painting Ruby and a list of colors used to paint Angelene. The first step in painting both carvings is to coat each figure in black primer. An inexpensive primer works best. We are using black primer to create the illusion that this piece has already had a long life and is a well established piece of Americana. When we scuff the paint overlying the primer to simulate wear, we want it to appear as if age-darkened wood is showing through, not shiny new basswood.

The latex paint colors we use on Ruby are Black, Antique Gold for the wings, Berry Red, and White. On Angelene, in addition to these colors use Flesh, Yellow (for the hair), and Baltic Blue for the eyes. On Ruby, the black primer acts as her skin color as well. The Black latex paint is used on Rudy to paint in the pupils of her eyes.

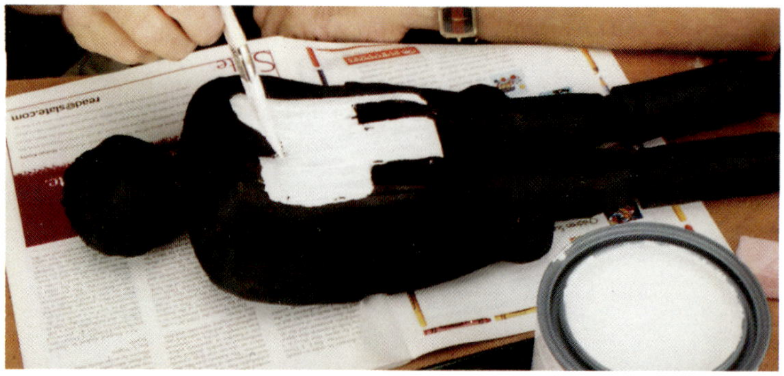

Painting Ruby's dress White.

Paint the upper arms and upper legs White to complete the dress. Paint the shoes and the fingernails red. Several coats of red will be needed to cover well.

Paint the wings Antique Gold.

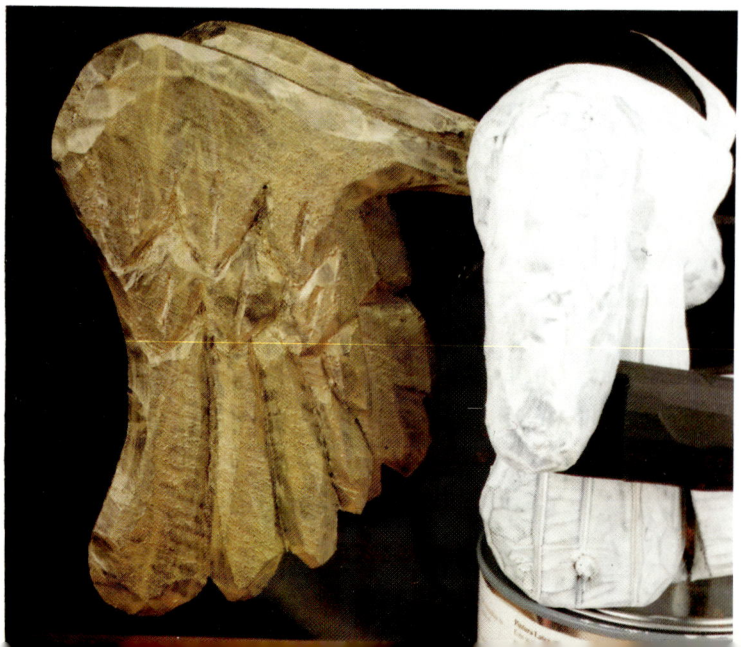

To create Ruby's face, paint two white ovals for eyes and add black pupils in the same location on each eye. Add red for the mouth and two red highlights for the cheeks. Scuff the paint lightly with 100 grit sandpaper. That allows the black primer to show through. Scuff the hair so the highlights of the dap show through. This scuffing highlights the high points on the carving marks and provides the appearance of age. Once the piece is scuffed, I apply a coat of dark brown Briwax to finish. This seals the paint and dulls down the colors a bit while also giving the piece a little sheen.

Gallery

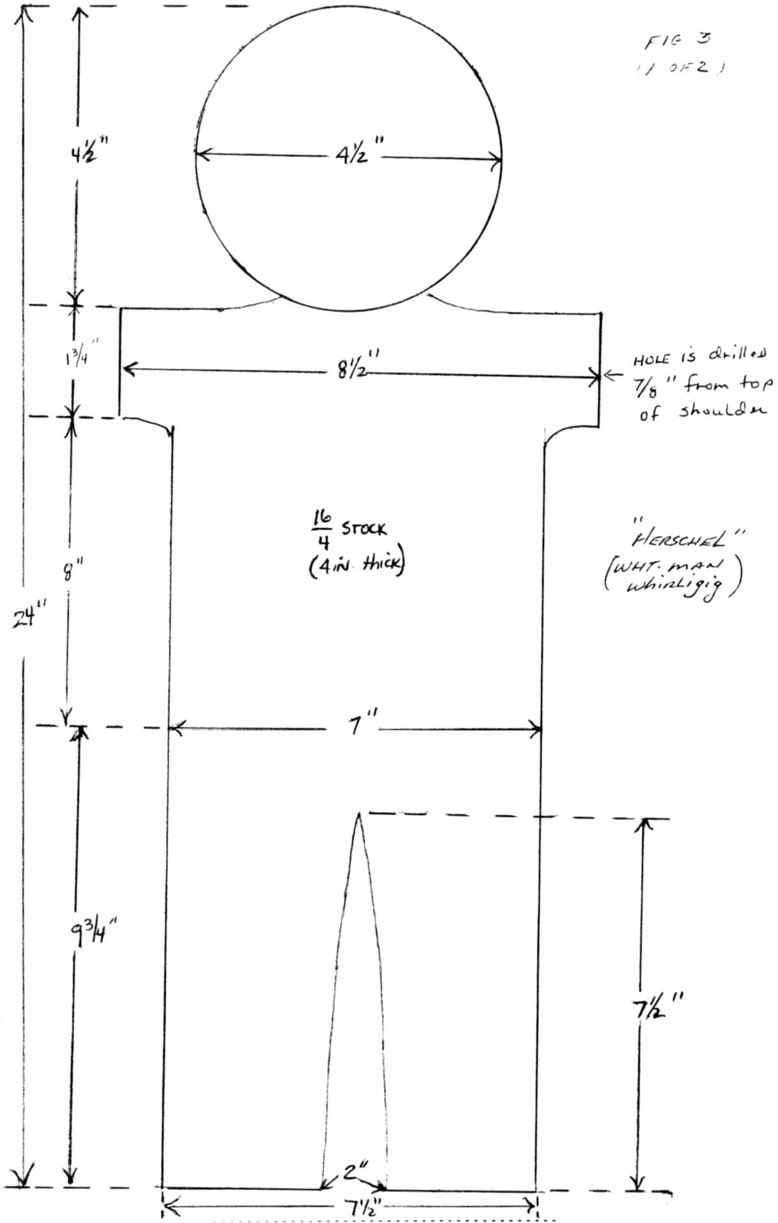

"Herschel" (wht. man whirligig).

Pattern shown reduced to 58%.

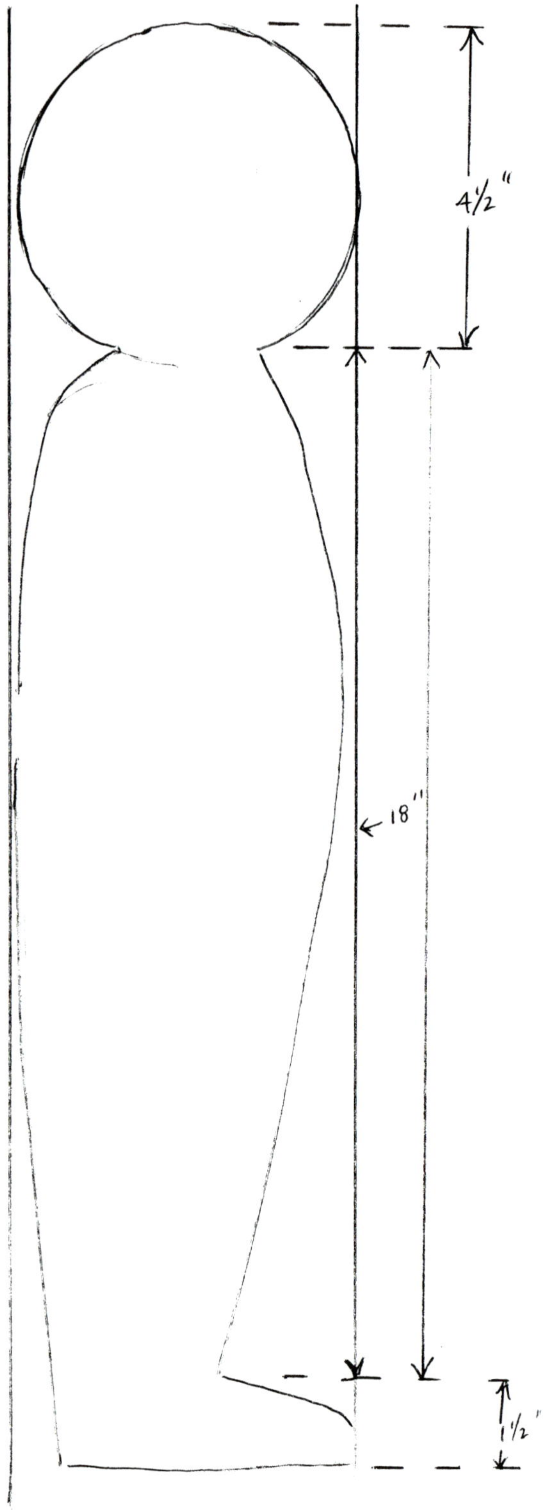

"Herschel" profile from 4" stock.

Pattern shown reduced to 75%.

When I was a boy in Tennessee, there was a man that came into town two or three times a year with a team of goats pulling a wagon. He had a white beard and would hold an auction in front of the courthouse — mainly with things he picked up along the way. Everybody called him the "Goatman." I never knew his name. When I was about fifteen, he quit passing through. No one ever saw him again. No one ever knew his name.

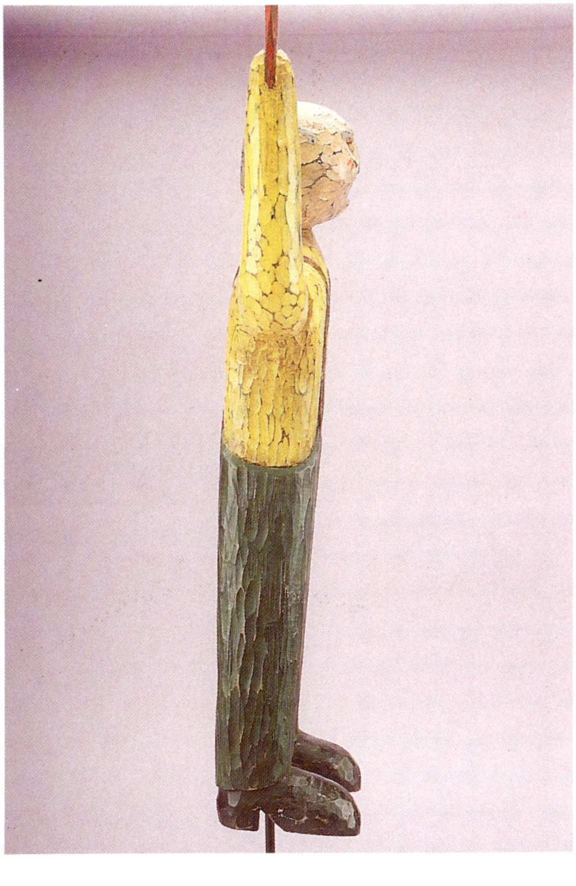

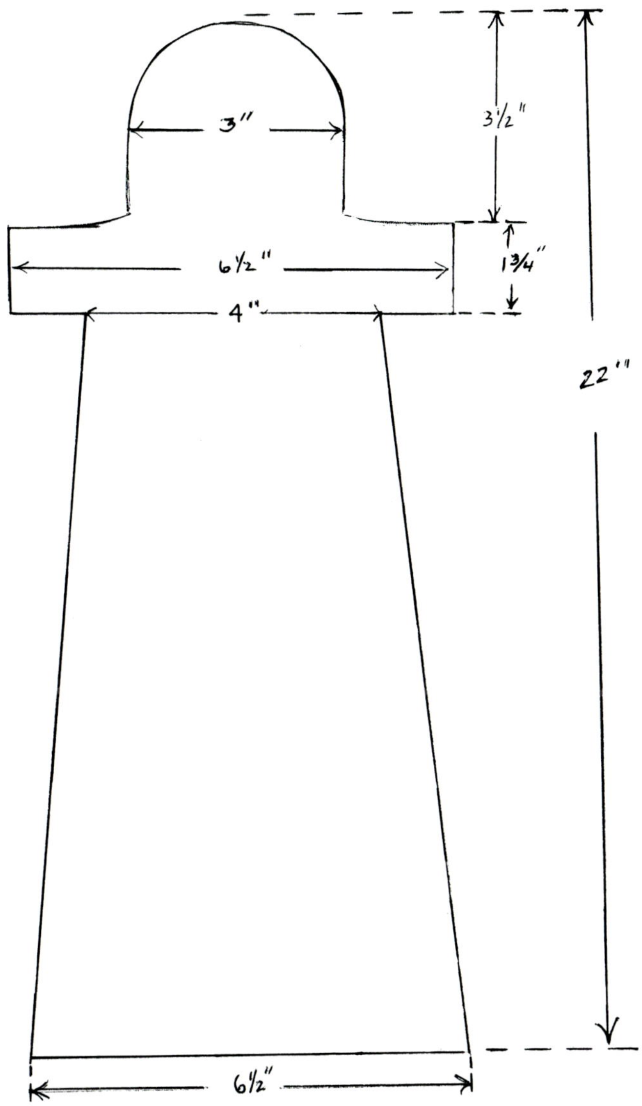

16/4 stock = 4" thick
"Noah" whirligig

Pattern shown reduced to 59%.

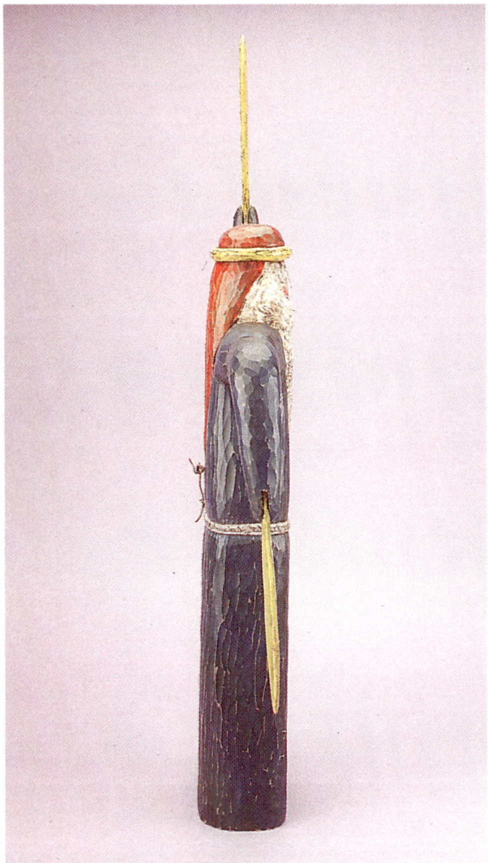

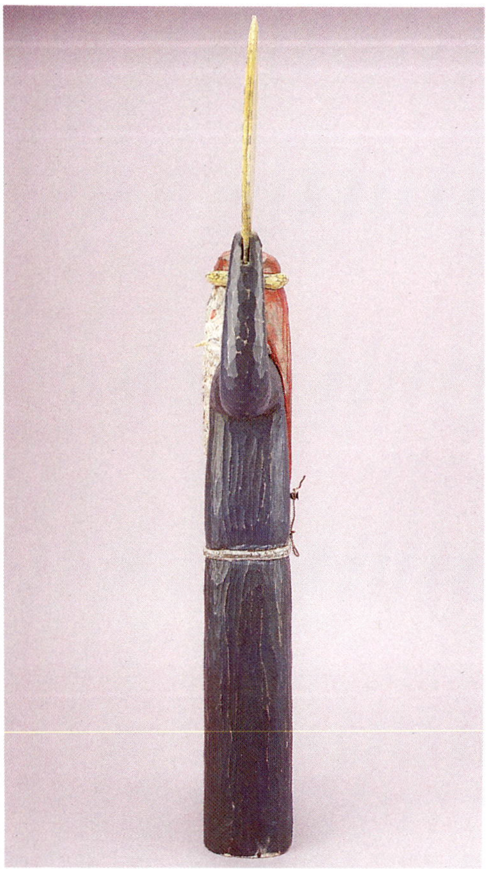

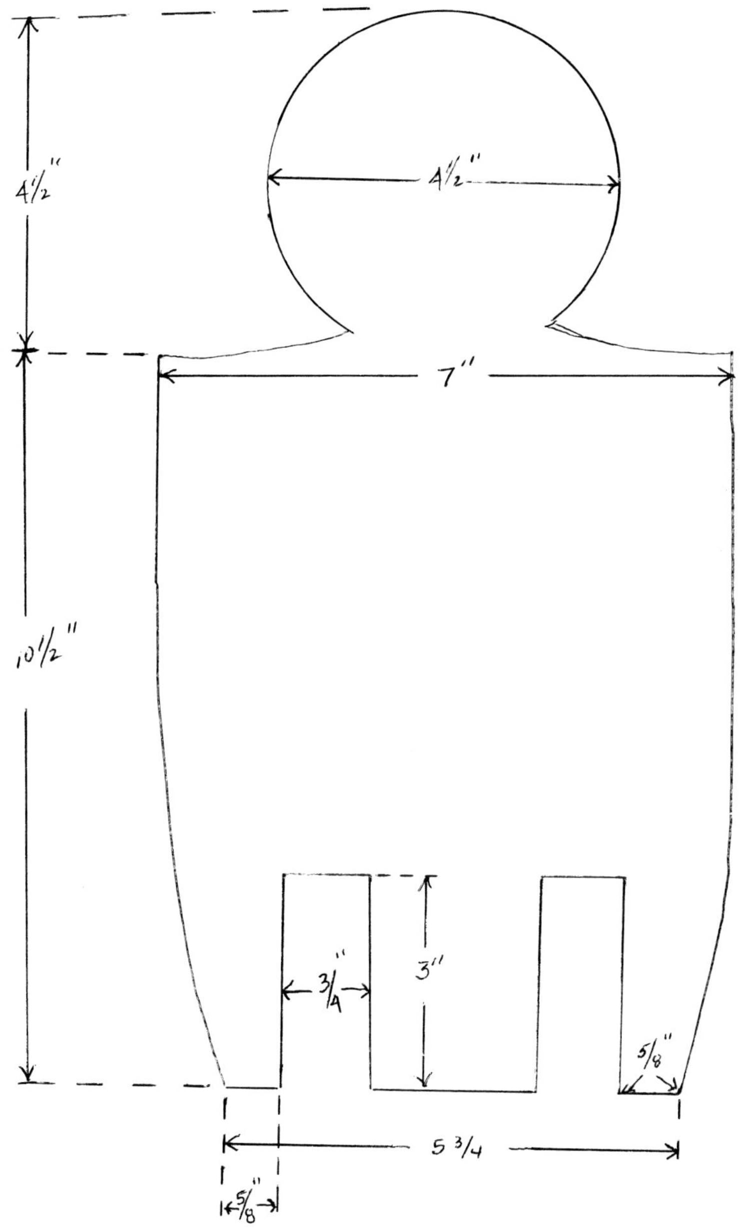

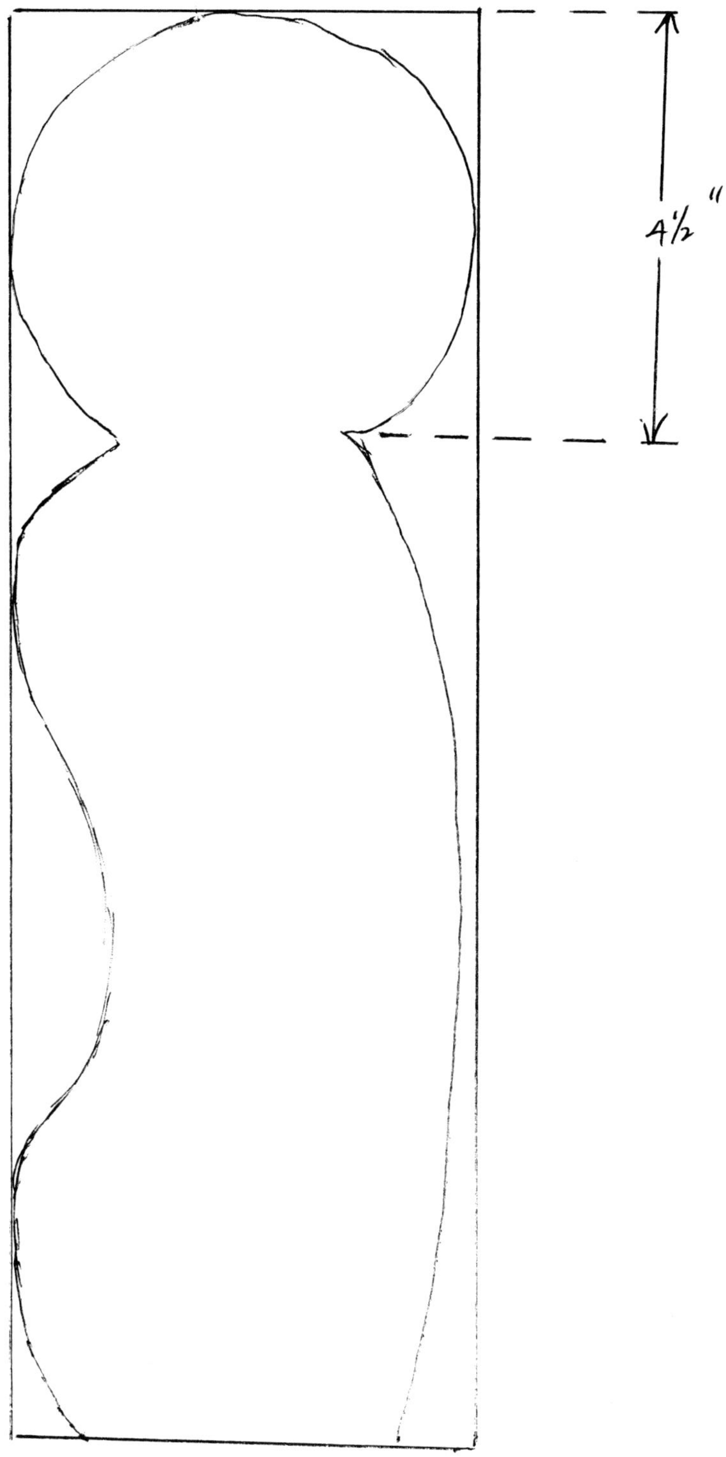

Lg. Articulated black man in Ministrial suit "Herschel".

Pattern shown reduced to 66%.

"Herschel" (Articulated) profile cut.

Pattern shown reduced to 87%.

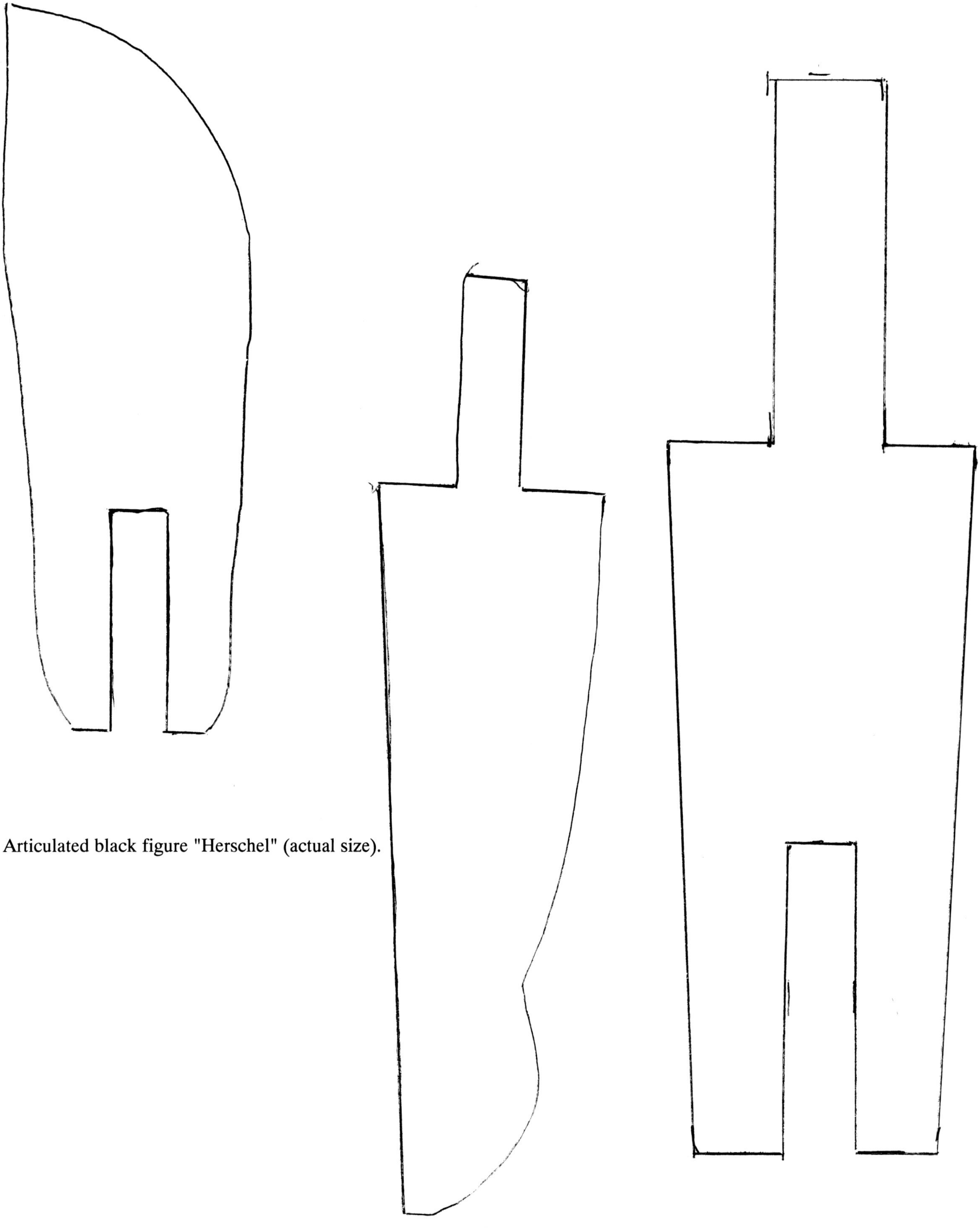

Articulated black figure "Herschel" (actual size).

Met a man years ago who was clearing land for twenty dollars an acre. He told me he had gone to free school a few days and could read his name but could not write it. Last I heard, he was a real estate developer.

Articulated black figure "Herschel" (actual size).

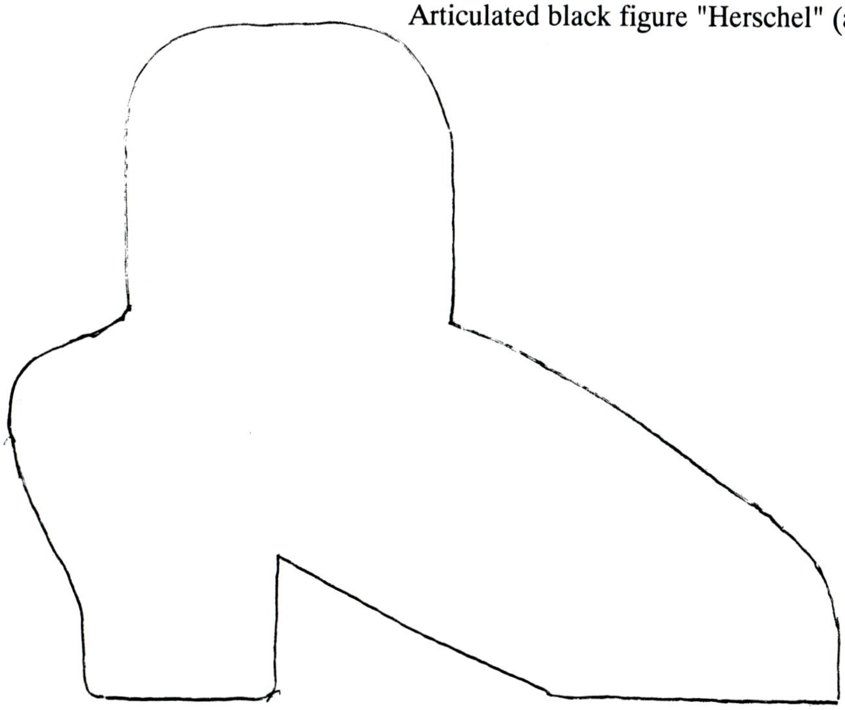

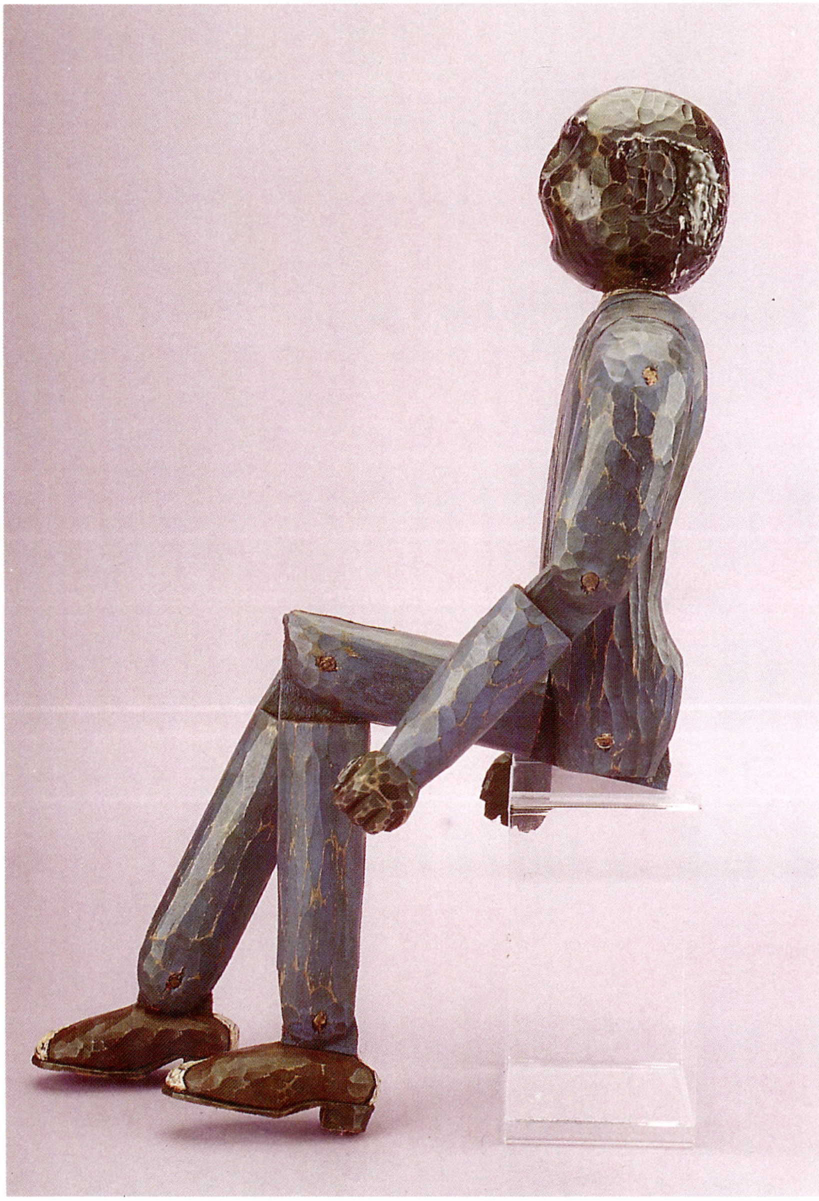

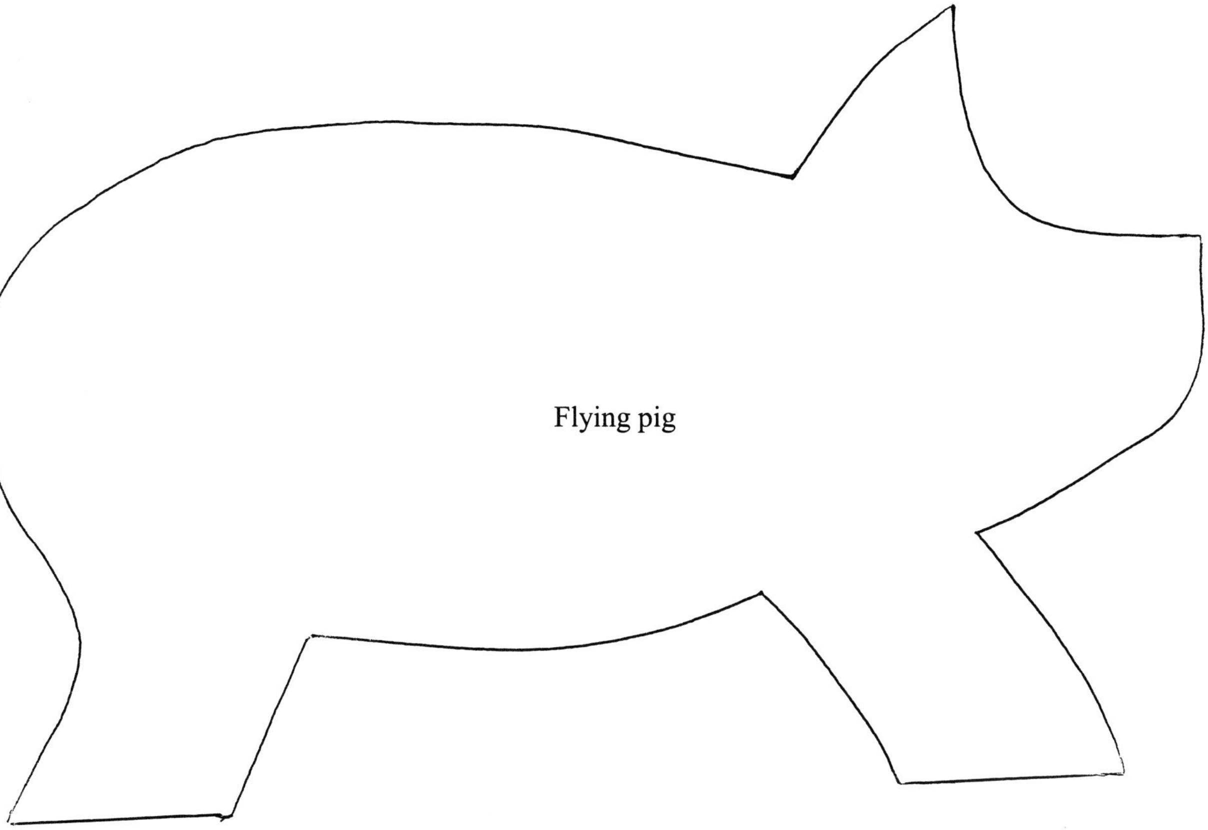

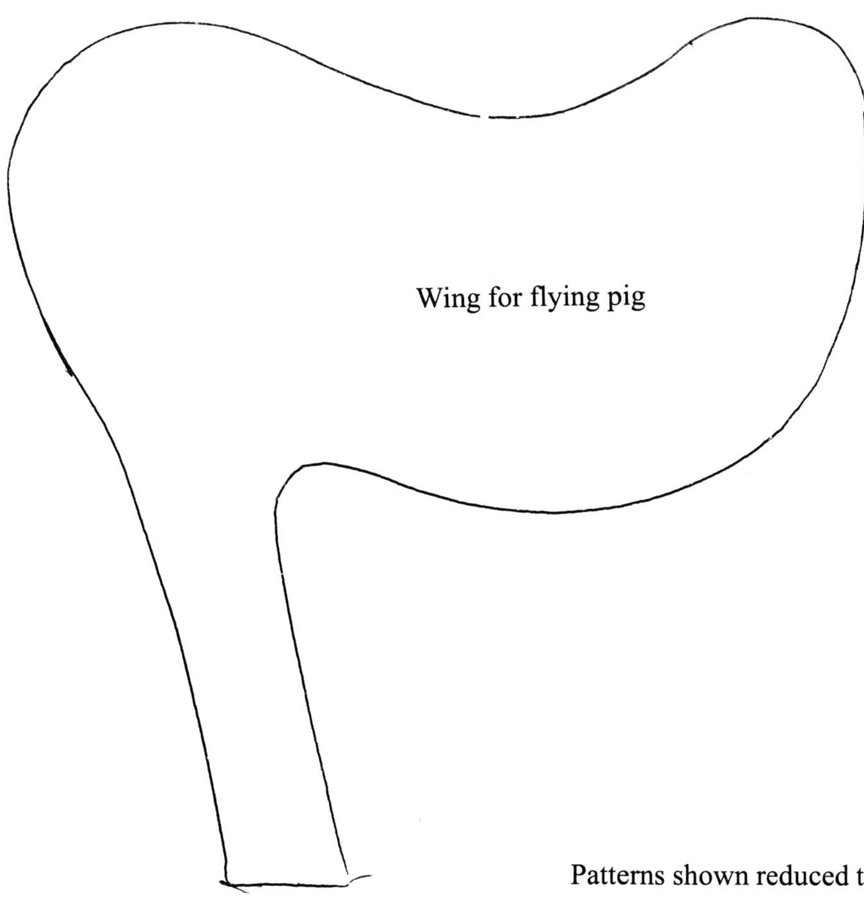

Patterns shown reduced to 75%.

Bought an old tin sign a while back ... all it said was "WE DON'T RENT PIGS."